All Year Round

*Exciting ideas for
peaceful playtimes*

JENNY MOSLEY
and GEORGIA THORP

Acknowledgements

I'm really pleased that since our early days of promoting playground projects – our first booklet for MDSAs was written in 1986 – we have finally pulled all the ideas together into one accessible and incredibly practical book. This has been thanks to Georgia's enthusiasm, creativity and tenacity – well done, Georgia!

Thank you also to my team of consultants who have been trialling and evaluating these ideas for the last ten years. Therese Hoyle has been a special Playground Pal. She has spent endless lunchtimes playing games, and has helped turn schools round by initiating positive playtime policies – real work!

These are exciting times to be in schools. There are wonderful people skipping and hula-hooping in a wild and joyous way all over the country!

Jenny Mosley

I should like to thank all the staff and children at Orchard, Rushmore and Gainsborough schools for letting me loose in their playgrounds to try out the ideas in this book.

Special thanks to the following. To Mandy Milsom, the head teacher at Gainsborough, for her trust, support and faith in me and the playtime model on our sometimes rocky road to improvement. To Abdi, who was in the very first group of the Gainsborough Friendship Squad and remained a member for four years. His enthusiasm and commitment, even when we were down to three children, was inspiring to us all. To my children, Zoe and Nicholas, who were both Friendship Squad members and told me where I was going wrong. To Andrew, my husband, who listened patiently to the daily triumphs and tribulations as I gathered information for this book.

Georgia Thorp

All Year Round
Exciting ideas for peaceful playtimes
LL01512
ISBN 1 85503 350 X
© Jenny Mosley and Georgia Thorp
Photography by George Solomonides
Illustrations by Mark Cripps
All rights reserved
First published 2002
Reprinted 2002, 2003

LDA, Duke Street, Wis ech, Cambs, PE13 2AE UK
3195 Wilson Drive NW, Grand Rapids, MI 49544 USA

Thanks to:
Gainsborough Primary School, for their invaluable support during the publication of this book
Sacred Heart School, Bells Hill, North Lanarkshire, for the use of their photographs.

The rights of Jenny Mosley and Georgia Thorp to be identified as authors of this work have been asserted by them in accordance with sections 77 and 78 of the Copyright, Designs and Patents Act 1988.

Copyright notice

Contents

Introduction

Do you recognise any of these scenarios? Does your school struggle to find solutions to them? If so, then this is the book you've been waiting for.

> *Mary Davis, head teacher, rubbed her temples. It was lunchtime, but there would be no break for her today, as usual. She probably wouldn't even manage a cup of tea, let alone anything to eat. The queue of 'naughty' children was already forming outside her door – the familiar faces that she saw with monotonous regularity. Lunchtimes were the bane of her life.*

> *Rosie James gazed listlessly at the crowd of children milling around the playground. She glanced at her watch – five minutes left. 'Bedlam,' she muttered to the other supervisor. 'Dinner ladies didn't have to put up with this when I was at school. It's no wonder nobody lasts long in this job.' She sighed. No point trying either. The PTA had provided the children with a box of lovely new games and equipment just a couple of months ago. It was all now lost, ruined or on the school's roof.*

> *Bob Hanley winced as he heard the bell announcing the end of lunchtime. He wondered what problems he would have to deal with today. It was a constant source of frustration that lunchtimes could produce so much misery. He resented the endless time wasted sorting out all the quarrels before the afternoon's teaching could begin.*

Ahmed had missed school often recently with stomach pains, but the doctor had discovered nothing wrong. Ahmed's mother was suspicious. Having learned from Ahmed's teacher that all was well in the classroom, she suspected that something was bothering her son about playtimes, but no amount of questioning would draw Ahmed on the subject.

Carly found the noise in the dining hall unbearable. She rarely ate all of her lunch because she was so desperate to escape it. Her afternoons were ruined by uncomfortable and distracting hunger pangs.

Sam hated playtimes. It wasn't so noticeable in the classroom that he had no friends, but in the playground he was alone. He didn't try to join in other children's games any more and didn't know what to do with himself. Most days he wandered around the edge of the playground wishing the bell would ring soon. That would end his boredom and isolation for another day.

Playtimes can be a source of tension and worry for children. If children are unhappy at playtime, they will be unhappy at school. A great deal of time and energy can be wasted by the children and the staff when they encounter negative experiences or have to deal with their consequences.

This book shows you how to:

- ▶ create happy and calm playtimes
- ▶ bring positive energy back into the school
- ▶ encourage children to play cooperatively
- ▶ support the adults involved in playtimes so they are equipped to support each other
- ▶ produce an outside environment that adults and children enjoy being in
- ▶ empower children to solve problems relating to playtimes.

What do I need to make the ideas work?

There are lots of ideas in this book that you can adapt to meet the specific needs of your school. Moreover, there is a strong emphasis on how to establish and develop a team ethos, which is vital for successful playtimes. In order to make the ideas in this book work, this is what you will need to do:

▶ Make **time** to explore and implement the ideas fully – this is the most important requirement. A good playtime policy takes time to develop.

▶ Use the following criteria to prioritise improvements by their importance to your school and how easy they are to implement.

▶ Help lunchtime supervisors become positive and enthusiastic by holding regular meetings with them to monitor progress and plan future developments. Ensure that they are paid for any additional working hours.

▶ Involve the whole school community, including governors, teachers, supervisors, support assistants, children and parents. Don't try to implement improvements, such as zoning the playground, without gaining general approval and enthusiasm.

▶ Consider holding an INSET day for all staff involved in playtimes.

▶ Include the children in any planning and decision-making. Use the school council and regular Circle Time sessions to discuss playtime issues and explore solutions.

▶ Work on a school development plan that includes well-structured, practical strategies for improving playtimes.

▶ Make sure that your school behaviour policy, with playtimes at its core, is discussed with parents. Use the school newsletter as a regular way to inform parents and to stimulate their support and interest.

▶ Incorporate developments into the curriculum; for example, children might learn about traditional games as part of History or PE.

▶ Make sure you plan a realistic budget for lunchtime improvements and their upkeep.

▶ Look at the budget allocations for PSHE and Citizenship, anti-bullying, special needs and positive behaviour, to see what can be used for playtimes, which are at the heart of all these areas.

▶ Assess how much additional funding you need to implement your plans and produce a fundraising programme. Approach the PTA and external groups for assistance.

▶ Gain the support of the wider community. For example, over-60s clubs, youth and community services, and secondary schools may be able to help in different ways.

How do I use this book?

The book provides a whole-school model, but each chapter can be used separately to help you implement specific improvements in your school. By focusing your efforts in a systematic way you can incorporate the whole framework. Every chapter provides you with an action plan that can be adapted to meet your school's individual requirements. Towards the end of the book there is a selection of photocopiable materials that are useful and practical resources.

How does this fit in with Circle Time?

We believe that Quality Circle Time (see Training and resources, page 198) is the ideal forum for helping children and adults to listen to, debate with and appreciate each other. Meetings may be held in a circle guided by agreed ground rules; for example, listen well, don't take issues personally, pay attention, and stay calm and positive. Weekly Circle Times help to create class and staff communities based on care and respect. Teachers can use Circle Time to explore children's feelings about playtimes, to develop solutions to problems and to teach playground games. At the end of the Circle Time the teacher can help the children to sum up the issues. They can then decide which of these need to be taken to the school council and which the teacher needs to take to a staff meeting that addresses playtimes. Staff need their own Circle Times to help each other with these issues too.

Whenever we, the Quality Circle Time team, use the phrase 'Circle Time', we are actually referring to an invisible circle of respect that needs to encompass a school to keep it emotionally safe. Creating effective playtime strategies is essential to keeping children physically and emotionally safe and enabling them to reach their full potential.

1 | *Raising the self-esteem and morale of supervisors*

When planning to improve your playtimes, the first responsibility of your school is to raise the self-esteem of your supervisors so that they feel valued, respected and more able to take on the challenge of changing systems and improving relationships. Some parents, children and occasionally even teaching staff see supervisors as 'second-class citizens'. Some children have this view because they never see supervisors (especially lunchtime supervisors) as part of school staff. The children experience their teachers as the powerful ones with dominant profiles who hold all the incentives, sanctions and resources. Lunchtime supervisors, on the other hand, often have low profiles, inferior or no incentives and sanctions, and no access to outside resources.

The following ideas will enable you to open up communication between staff, identify areas your school needs to address to help change attitudes and perceptions, and raise the self-esteem and profile of your supervisors.

School prospectus

When you draw up your school prospectus, make sure you include a section about playtimes, including the names of supervisors and commenting on the important contributions they make to school life.

Welcome board

Some schools have a board in their entrance hall with photographs and names of all school staff, including the catering and lunchtime staff, and a cheerful message welcoming visitors to their school.

School newsletter

If your school has a newsletter, make sure that all staff receive a copy, and that supervisors and catering staff have a regular mention. You could focus on a specific aspect of playtime, or ask a child to interview a lunchtime supervisor about the highs and lows of a typical lunchtime at school.

Curriculum

Try putting up a display about supervisors in the hall or a classroom. The children can interview supervisors about a typical school day. They could draw pictures of supervisors and write poems about what they think they do or what it would be like if there were no supervisors in the playground or dining hall.

Leaflet on playtimes and lunchtimes for parents and carers

Use a summary of the playtime and lunchtime policy to inform parents and carers about:

▶   your playtimes and lunchtimes
▶   rules, routines, rewards and sanctions
▶   who your supervisors are and what their role is.

Staffroom pigeon holes

Many staffrooms have pigeon holes for passing on information to other teachers; can this be extended in your school to include supervisors?

Staff notice board

Include information on training courses and other relevant information, for all staff. Lunchtime supervisors often feel that they are the last people to get such information.

Day book

Keep a book in the staffroom, or another place that is easily accessible to supervisors, with any issues they need to be aware of written in it. For example, a child may be having problems at home and need some support. Staff are much more likely to be sympathetic towards a child if they know such details.

Morning meetings

Invite a representative from the supervisors to your morning meetings. They can then pass on any relevant information to colleagues.

Medical conditions

Keep a book recording the names of children with medical conditions whom supervisors need to be aware of. Keep it in an accessible place.

Social events

When you organise a social event make sure the invitation is extended to all staff. Make opportunities for supervisors to suggest and help organise events and activities, giving them a sense of being part of the process, rather than inviting them as an afterthought.

Meetings

Establish regular monthly or half-termly meetings, as these provide an opportunity for supervisors to:

▶ be listened to

▶ discuss ideas and improvements

▶ highlight current problems and suggest possible solutions

▶ have a chance to meet other supervisors in a relaxed atmosphere, developing understanding and tolerance

▶ feel that their ideas and suggestions matter

▶ develop a sense of worth

▶ have fun.

Meetings are best led by someone with particular responsibilities for lunchtimes and playtimes. This is usually the head teacher or deputy. The meetings should be time-tabled and promoted in advance, with all staff reminded on the day.

> *How come our meeting isn't written on the staff notice board, isn't it important enough?*
>
> Supervisor

Sometimes teachers don't acknowledge the importance and value of the meetings. It is essential that teaching staff appreciate the problems faced by supervisors and they should be encouraged to affirm supervisors in the way they talk to and about them.

Written minutes of meetings pinned on the staff notice board highlight their importance and give teaching staff a chance to see what the issues are.

Your first meeting will primarily be to listen to the concerns and anxieties supervisors have. There are always considerable resentments and grumbles, but it is important at this stage to listen sympathetically in a non-defensive way. Subsequent sessions can be structured around the issues raised. The framework and action plans throughout the book will help to address the different areas. There are training sessions in chapter 5 that you can use as a starting point. 'Guidelines for good relationships between children and lunchtime supervisors' (see page 70–71) will help you to establish a set of agreed guidelines for playtimes and enable everyone to become familiar with the behaviour expected from staff towards children and each other.

Remember that your meetings should take a problem-solving approach and should not become sessions for blaming and criticising, with no ideas for improvements or solutions.

When to have your meetings

This varies from school to school. Some lunchtime supervisors are also classroom assistants, whilst others are only on duty during lunchtime. We have found the best time for the meetings to be just after lunchtime. The atmosphere is much more relaxed then. Meetings of at least an hour are needed and should take place in a comfortable room (many schools use their staffroom). For some supervisors this is the only time they come into the school building, apart from lunchtime and wet playtime. Providing a warm, welcoming and friendly environment with some light refreshments is a small way of showing that you value your supervisors, and helps create a positive and relaxed atmosphere.

Assembly

At the beginning of each half-term, a whole-school assembly which focuses on the playground and lunchtime rules, routines, rewards and sanctions will help remind the children of behaviour expected. Supervisors are invited to these assemblies not only as an important part of raising their profile as members of the school community, but also to give them an opportunity for active participation. The latter can be a very daunting experience for some but should be gently encouraged where possible. One suggestion is to invite supervisors to present lunchtime reward certificates (see Training and resources, page 199) on a termly basis. Another might be to ask supervisors to say one thing they feel has improved at lunchtimes.

Staff development and training

Enabling staff to develop and learn new skills will help them to realise their potential, build their confidence and raise their self-esteem. Local Education Authorities or consultancy companies offer training sessions and courses on managing difficult behaviour, conflict resolution, anger management and first aid. One advantage of training is that it gives staff an opportunity to meet supervisors from other schools to share ideas. This will help them reflect on their practice and how their school manages different situations. It may also help them to realise that their school is doing well after all.

Having a commitment to improving and developing playtimes in your school needs to be reflected in your school development plan. Money should be budgeted for the professional development of supervisors and any extra meetings they may attend. You will also need to fund supply cover for a teacher who may be involved in meetings or training sessions with supervisors.

INSET

INSET is a valuable opportunity to involve supervisors as part of the process, sharing ownership of training in certain areas and also policy development. In particular, involve them in the development of your behaviour and anti-bullying policy, which should focus on agreeing and sharing fundamental aims and values and should deal specifically with:

▶ strategies used
▶ preventive measures
▶ promoting positive behaviour
▶ managing confrontation
▶ understanding difficult children.

We have been in schools where the behaviour and anti-bullying policy has been written by senior management teams and teachers without any input from supervisors. In fact, supervisors very often have no idea of what is in the policy because they have never been given a copy of it.

Whole-school INSET can help to bridge the gap (which can be quite big in some schools) not only between supervisors and teaching staff, but between supervisors and supervisors. It creates opportunities for all staff to work together and enables people to get to know each other without the pressure of a normal school day. A day spent together can help break down barriers and alter attitudes and preconceived ideas about colleagues.

> *He's alright once you get to know him. I didn't know he was so funny until we had the time to talk.*
>
> Two supervisors
> talking about a teacher

Induction for new supervisors

Some schools have a staff handbook on playtimes for all supervisors. This is a very useful way for new staff to familiarise themselves with the daily routines of their role.

Making a new member of staff feel welcome as early as possible in your school and as part of your team is very important to the smooth running of your systems. It can be a very daunting experience for a new member of staff with no support to go into the playground; there they may feel like the 'new child'. They have not yet familiarised themselves with the routine or got to know the other supervisors. Asking a supervisor to mentor new staff and shadow them for a short time until they feel confident will help them integrate into school life and routines quickly and gently.

Class Circle Times

Invite supervisors to attend those Circle Times that review playtimes in the classroom context. Supervisors and the teacher can talk about things that are going well with the children and help to identify problems in the playground. They can discuss and think of ideas to improve these situations.

Teacher's role

Some schools have a brief handover at the beginning or end of lunchtime. This is an ideal time for teacher and supervisor to share any relevant information about the children. Perhaps the teacher needs to tell the supervisor to be aware of a conflict that developed in class, or the supervisor may need to inform the teacher about a child who is feeling unwell. This handover reinforces the value the teacher places on the supervisor's role. Similarly, arriving promptly to collect children from the playground illustrates the teacher's appreciation of the supervisor.

Link supervisors to specific classes

It may be possible to link a supervisor with one or two classes on a termly basis. They can visit those classes and discuss playground successes and problems. Some teachers have a 'tell a good tale' discussion after lunchtime, where they ask some children and the supervisor to share something positive about lunchtime. This will promote the key role of the supervisor in the smooth running of the school.

Playtime and lunchtime policy

Develop a clear playtime and lunchtime policy with the help of your supervisors, using the ideas and strategies discussed and developed from the training sessions and meetings (see chapter 5). Share this with the wider school community, including children, staff, governors and parents. This will help you to set out clear aims and objectives in line with your behaviour and anti-bullying policies. It will also enable you to identify training needs for your staff.

CASE STUDY

One primary school's approach to establishing regular meetings with supervisors, 1998–2001

We have six lunchtime supervisors, four of whom are full-time and are also employed as teaching assistants; one works part-time and one works only during lunchtimes. One of the supervisors has been working in the school for 25 years and others have between 7 and 18 years' service. Our newest recruit, with only one year's service, is the daughter of a supervisor! The supervisors' ages range from 28 to 55. Many have had their own children at the school and live locally in a tight-knit community, where they have close contact with many of the parents and children outside school.

Having recently attended one of Jenny Mosley's Quality Circle Time courses on improving playtimes, I was keen and enthusiastic to share my new-found knowledge on improving playtimes in our school. This was an issue because there was fighting, conflict and little regard or respect for the adults in the playground.

My first task was to organise an initial meeting with the supervisors, to which I invited the head teacher. This was to be the first of many meetings and indeed was the first time ever that a formal meeting for the supervisors had been organised. I was a little apprehensive, to say the least.

I began the meeting by asking staff to complete the statements, *One thing I like about playtime is …* and *One thing I don't like about playtime is …*

They struggled to complete the sentences, but typical answers included *I can't think of anything that I like*, *I like the free dinner I get*, *I suppose a child making me laugh because of what they said*.

I used a wooden egg as our 'talking object' (only the person holding the egg is allowed to speak). The session was quite restrained, with the more dominant characters making the greatest contribution. Having the egg did make it more difficult for individuals to interrupt and the quieter members were able to contribute to some degree.

The aims for the first meeting were:

▶ to bring everyone together and make the supervisors feel valued by listening to their concerns

➡

CASE STUDY

▶ to discuss the idea of improving playtime behaviour by merging the Key Stage 1 and Key Stage 2 playgrounds

▶ to introduce the idea of activity zones (see chapter 6).

The last two aims were met with uncertainty and a general lack of enthusiasm. The concern was that if children were allowed to play anywhere in the playground the older children would hurt the younger ones – not always on purpose, but with the general rough and tumble of play this would be inevitable. They said that the parents 'won't have it'. They also found it hard to understand the concept of zoning and how it was going to work.

I agreed that if we did the merging in isolation from everything else in the playground then the supervisors' misgivings would be well founded.

It was clear from what the supervisors said that the ethos of the playground was quite different from that within the school building, and that it operated as a law unto itself. In the past, dialogue with the head teacher only occurred if there was a problem, or if there was something specific the supervisors needed to know. This apparently suited them, or at least this is what they had become used to. In one person's words, 'We were left to sort out the playground problems.' Between them they had 60 years' service at the school and had evolved their own system and strategies, which until now had been very much their responsibility.

There wasn't an official hierarchy, but there were clear leaders within the group. There was no senior supervisor with overall responsibility for lunchtimes, there never had been and that was the way it was going to stay! However, I needed someone in the playground I could liaise with, who would act as a link, helping to monitor progress and note any concerns. The relationships and dynamics of this group had a long history that I was not party to. This was not an easy problem to overcome, but with time the supervisors became more forthcoming. A turning point came when two supervisors volunteered to support the Friendship Squad.

Subsequent meetings have taken place every half-term and are planned for an hour after a lunchtime. I bring in fruit juice and cake (home made if I have time to cook). These meetings often run over time. The head teacher occasionally attends, but I have found that the supervisors are more open if the head teacher is not there. We enjoy the meetings, and in the first year we began to make steady progress towards developing links with each other and the teaching staff.

→

The meetings have given the supervisors the opportunity to express their views, raise issues and look at ways of working together to address them. They have become a forum for discussing problems and finding group solutions, which has helped overcome a feeling of powerlessness. Recently we had to cancel a meeting and one supervisor said, 'I was really looking forward to that meeting!'

The majority of our supervisors are also classroom assistants, so they have been working in school when we have had meetings. Funds were set aside to pay those who attended these meetings outside their normal working hours.

We introduced the reward and sanction system explored in *Turn Your School Round* (see Training and resources, page 199), in which we record positive and negative behaviour at playtimes on red and yellow notelets, which the supervisors give out. These notelets are passed on to the class teachers at the end of playtime. This enables the supervisors to have access to rewards and sanctions in line with our whole-school approach to behaviour management. One difficulty in establishing this system has been the supervisors' lack of consistency in using the notelets. Some are very keen and give out lots of positive notelets, others give out mainly ' I am disappointed' notelets and some don't use them at all. Keeping it going and reminding the supervisors that they are major contributors to the positive ethos in the playground has been difficult at times.

Practical playground management has played a large part in the strategy. For example, through the meetings we agreed to have a first-aid bag in the playground to overcome the problem of supervisors having to leave the playground to administer first aid, leaving the playground understaffed.

Other practical concerns dealt with included:

▶ not knowing which teachers were on duty
▶ not being told if visitors were going to be in the playground
▶ teachers' and supervisors' authority being undermined, sometimes by children playing one off against the other
▶ child protection issues.

I have a meeting with the head teacher to discuss issues which are not resolved at the meeting and report back to staff next time, or before if it is a matter of urgency.

CASE STUDY

CASE STUDY

Three years later, 2001

Through our regular meetings we have worked very hard to build a positive relationship with support staff and teachers. It has been difficult to achieve at times, but we are proud that three years on we have accomplished the following:

▶ regular meetings where supervisors are forthcoming about finding solutions to problems

▶ the writing up of minutes that are distributed to supervisors and put on the staff notice board

▶ supervisors taking part in training sessions on behaviour and anti-bullying and in staff Circle Times

▶ the outside first-aid kit has been replaced with individual bum bags for supervisors to prevent children helping themselves to first-aid equipment (this had a very affirming effect in a recent staff meeting when two supervisors demonstrated the very different contents of their bum bags, which created mass hysteria amongst the group)

▶ a lunchtime policy and a staff handbook for supervisors

▶ a leaflet for parents on playtime rules and routines.

Our meetings will be effective as long as we continue to work together to build a strong team spirit that will enable the change and improvement process to continue. We need to be able to trust and support each other and to be consistent in our approach to dealing with issues and systems that we have established. We need regularly to review and adapt our ideas to meet the needs of our school.

RAISING THE SELF-ESTEEM AND MORALE OF THE SUPERVISORS

Task	Have you:	Resources you may need	Person responsible/ monitored by	Estimated cost	Review date
Raise the profile of supervisors	• included a section in the school prospectus about your supervisors and the job they do? • drawn up a list of supervisors and the important contribution they make in school? • put up a welcome board with photos and names of your supervisors?	• information about your supervisors • list of names • welcome board			
Develop a system which informs supervisors of day-to-day events	• set up a system to ensure all supervisors receive/see information about training, courses and newsletters? • used the newsletter to give supervisors a regular mention? • set up a system which informs supervisors of day-to-day issues about individual children who need extra support? • invited supervisors to morning meetings?	• notebook • notice board • pigeon holes			
Organise inclusive social events	• invited supervisors to help to organise social events? • asked supervisors to organise an event?				

Task	Have you:	Resources you may need	Person responsible/ monitored by	Estimated cost	Review date
Instigate meetings	• identified someone who will take responsibility for running the meetings? • timetabled half-termly or monthly meetings? • informed teachers about the meetings? • decided on the best time to hold your meetings? • decided where they will take place? • made refreshments available? • adopted a problem-solving approach? • used the sessions to look at specific areas needing improvement?	• minutes of the meeting with action notes for attention by the following meeting			
Hold half-termly assemblies about playtime and lunchtime	• organised a half-termly assembly to reinforce the school rules and expected behaviour, which the supervisors are invited to attend and take part in?	• budget to cover costs of attending assembly			
Organise staff training and development	• given opportunities to supervisors to attend: courses and training sessions run by Local Education Authorities? INSET training sessions on whole-staff and supervisor training?	• budget to cover costs of attending sessions			

RAISING THE SELF-ESTEEM AND MORALE OF THE SUPERVISORS

Task	Have you:	Resources you may need	Person responsible/ monitored by	Estimated cost	Review date
Induction for new staff	• a supervisors' staff handbook? • a mentor to shadow new staff?	• supervisors' handbook			
Find other ways of raising supervisors' profile	• asked teaching staff to invite supervisors to Circle Time sessions about playtimes? • linked supervisors with classes to enable them to pop into a class with feedback? • organised formal handovers as children line up at the end of lunchtime, so the supervisors can share information about the children with the teachers? • encouraged teachers to explain the importance of the supervisor's role to the children? • made a display about the supervisors, written and drawn by the children?	• notebook • notice board • pigeon holes • materials for display			

→

Task	Have you:	Resources you may need	Person responsible/ monitored by	Estimated cost	Review date
Agree on and write playtime and lunchtime policy	• consulted the supervisors in the development of the policy? • developed a policy with clear aims and objectives? • linked it to the behaviour and anti-bullying policies? • summarised it in leaflet form for parents?	• meetings with supervisors • sample policies • leaflet for parents			

2 | *Creating rules, incentives and sanctions that work*

This chapter focuses on establishing clear rules, incentives and sanctions to support the improvement of playtimes in your school.

Playground rules

It is essential that the moral ethos of the playground is linked to that within the school. Playground rules embody the behaviour that the children are encouraged to practise. These are discussed and agreed with staff and children and are displayed in the playground. Displaying the rules helps to inform all members of the school community and visitors of your moral values and clear expectations of behaviour.

Whatever rules are decided upon, the focus is on what we *should* do rather than what we *shouldn't* do. The rules below offer a good starting point.

Golden Playground Rules

Golden Rules are the moral values or vision that unite the whole school. These are:

- Do be gentle, don't hurt anybody
- Do be kind and helpful, don't hurt others' feelings
- Do be honest, don't cover up the truth
- Do look after property, don't waste or damage things
- Do play cooperatively, don't spoil people's fun
- Do listen to people, don't interrupt.

Schools we have worked with display their Golden Rules and Playground Rules next to each other.

You may want to have specific rules that focus on particular routines that are expected from the children. An example follows.

Five rules for a happy playtime

● When the bell rings we stand still.

● We play together and look after each other.

● We let other children get on with their own games.

● We give the equipment to the Playground Friends at the end of playtime.

● We tell an adult if we feel sad or lonely.

Safety rules

Once your rules are large and evident in the dining hall and playground, it is important that your team of supervisors, in consultation with the teachers, works out the 'nitty gritty' safety rules that apply specifically to these areas.

These rules also need to be large and should be displayed next to your playtime rules. Safety rules include guidance such as:

● Don't play behind the bushes

● Only use soft balls

● Don't run in the quiet zone

● Don't spit.

Incentives and sanctions

Developing incentives

A clear incentive and sanctions system is an integral part of your playtime improvements and will help reinforce your playtime systems. It will also enable supervisors to uphold their status and authority with the children. A meeting to discuss what incentives and sanctions are available in your school would be a good starting point.

If your school has no playtime incentives for staff to use, this is an ideal opportunity to discuss and agree some ideas from this section. When staff have chosen what they will try, it is more likely to be successful because they have played a part in the decision-making and have a sense of ownership. Monitoring and reviewing the system is the key to its success.

Mini-certificates

Staff have mini-certificates in a bright colour (we suggest yellow), with a list of different behaviours written on each underneath the phrase 'I am pleased with you because you chose to ...' (see page 171).

The supervisors tick and sign the behaviour they are commending a child for on the mini-certificate, and either give it directly to the child or to the teacher at the end of playtime when classes are lining up. Some schools link these mini-certificates with their classroom incentives. For example, a mini-certificate on the playground is exchanged for a merit or points for their class team, thus integrating the playground incentive system with that of the whole school. Some teachers put the certificates up on their class celebration board for a few days before the children take them home; others allow the children to take them home immediately.

> *I watched a boy giving his mother a certificate and she shouted 'I want to see more of these, this is what makes me happy!' His beaming smile said it all! This was a child who was always getting into trouble and the news she usually got was bad.*
>
> Teacher

'I am pleased with you' book or monitoring form

Staff can nominate children by adding their names to the book or form (see page 172). These children are mentioned in assembly. If your school has a whole-school achievement board their names can also be added to this.

Good lunchtime certificate

Lunchtime supervisors can give out certificates praising good behaviour (see Training and resources, page 199) to all children who did not receive an 'I am disappointed' notelet during the course of the term.

Stickers

Staff have a range of stickers with phrases like 'Well done for being kind' which they give to children. These are available from LDA (see Training and resources, page 199).

Raffle

This is a weekly raffle in which tickets are given to children by lunchtime supervisors for keeping a playtime rule. At the end of each week a number is pulled out of the box in assembly and the child whose number is drawn gets a prize. Children are encouraged to say which rule they kept.

End of play

Some schools have real problems with children taking too long to line up after playtime. Supervisors can give out tokens or tickets to every class that lines up within the agreed time. These may be exchanged for class merits or other whole-class rewards.

Feeling part of the whole

Some schools link supervisors with one or two classes on a termly basis. They visit these classes regularly and share any good news or problems the class may be having at playtime. This will encourage a closer and more understanding relationship with the teacher and children in that class.

Sanctions

Despite having well-organised playtimes and incentives, there will always be a minority of children who do not respond and a clear sanction system will help them to understand the consequences if the school rules are broken.

Being zoned

If your school has zoned activity areas you can use zoning as a sanction. Children who consistently break the school rules have to stay in a particular zone for a specified period of time. This helps keep some children apart and minimises conflicts.

Help cards

These are cards that all supervisors carry and use if they need assistance from inside the school. They can send a child in with a card. Some schools have a rota system for members of teaching and management staff on lunchtime duty, so that someone is always available to give help.

Loss of Golden Time

Golden Time is an occasion each week when all children who have kept the Golden Rules have a special time to do a range of activities. If they break the rules they have part of their Golden Time taken away.

If your school has Golden Time as part of its incentives and sanctions policy, you may want to link it to your playtime sanctions. If a child has had a verbal warning and continues to break a playground rule their name will be forwarded to the teacher and they lose part of their Golden Time. There can be a reluctance for some schools to link the playtime and class sanctions. The main reason is that the class teacher may feel that playground issues should be kept in the playground and not spill into the classroom, where they have to 'punish' a child for something they have not witnessed.

'I am disappointed' notelets

These are little notelets easily distinguishable from the 'I am pleased with you' mini-certificates (see page 18). A list of negative behaviours is written underneath the phrase 'I am disappointed that, having given you a verbal warning, you still chose to ...' (see page 173 for photocopiable notelets).

A notelet can be used after a child has been given a verbal warning for breaking a rule. If they persist in breaking it then a notelet can be filled in. The notelets can be put in a special box, or the details can be transferred to an 'I am disappointed with your behaviour', monitoring form (see page 174) which is kept in a place easily accessible to supervisors. The box or monitoring form is checked on a regular basis and children whose names appear more than an agreed number of times are invited to see the head teacher.

Example of a sanction system

1 The child is given a verbal warning and told what rule they have broken. They choose how they will continue to behave. Giving them a choice encourages them to take responsibility for their own behaviour.

2 If they continue to break the rule, their name is written on an 'I am disappointed' notelet.

3 This goes into the 'I am disappointed box', which is kept in the staffroom.

4   Each week the head teacher empties the box. If a name appears more than twice in a week that child is invited to see the head teacher to discuss the problem.

5   The head teacher works with the child to set some playtime targets which will be monitored on a daily basis within a time frame (usually one or two weeks). The child chooses a supervisor to whom they agree to go if they have any problems at playtime. Having a named supervisor will help to build a positive supportive relationship between them.

6   The supervisor is given the child's playground target card (see page 175), which has up to three targets written on it. At the end of playtime the supervisor will sign a happy or sad face on the back of the sheet (see page 176), depending on whether the child has managed to keep their targets. This continues for the agreed time.

7   When the child meets their playground targets, a celebratory Well Done certificate (see page 177) is sent home and they are able to go out and resume normal playtime activities.

8   If there are no improvements, a letter will be sent home explaining what has happened and asking the parents or carers to come in and discuss the problem with a view to finding a way of working. A reward system that will be reinforced at home could be agreed. For example, when the child has kept their playground targets and taken a Well Done certificate home, they will be rewarded with a treat such as a small toy or a trip to the cinema.

9   If the child refuses to cooperate after a range of sanctions has been tried the only option may be lunchtime exclusion.

To summarise:

1   Verbal warning

2   'I am disappointed' notelet

3   Transferred to 'I am disappointed' box

4   Box emptied at the end of each week

5   Head teacher and child set playground targets

6   Supervisor signs playground targets card

7   Well Done certificate is sent home

8   If no improvement, parents or carers are involved.

Beyond the usual sanctions

If a child verbally or physically attacks a member of staff or pupil, the details are recorded on an Incident form. The adult involved, or who witnessed the behaviour, writes down what happened. The child is invited into the head teacher's office, where the form is read out. They are asked if they agree with the details and then to sign the form. The parents of the child are notified. Sanctions employed could include suspension from playtimes or school exclusion, as well as a specific programme to help the child change their behaviour.

At the beginning of a term some head teachers like to note key information from the Incident forms, take the original forms into an assembly and tear them up as a symbolic fresh start for the children involved.

The child beyond

When we talk about the 'child beyond' we are referring to the sort of child who is beyond the normal incentives and sanctions system.

Having put in place many of the strategies outlined in this book to promote a caring playground and to encourage good behaviour, we may find that there are a minority of children who have deep emotional problems and need very clear boundaries set within a highly supportive framework. These children find it very difficult to manage playtimes without constantly becoming involved in fights and other conflict situations. They are sent out into the playground and expected to manage. When they fail to do so, they are punished.

The following ideas will help you to develop programmes for these children on the verge of exclusion. These ideas may enable them to:

- build relationships with their peers and adults in school
- raise their self-esteem
- develop skills to help them have positive experiences at playtimes.

It is important to provide an appropriate support system that allows the responsibility for supporting these children to be shared between all members of staff and not left to the supervisors.

Target specific behaviours

All children on these programmes will have a playground target card (see page 175) that is signed at the end of each playtime to show whether they have managed to achieve their targets. These are regularly reviewed and when a child achieves their targets they have a Well Done certificate (see page 177) signed by their teacher, which is sent home. Alternatively, if a child is not managing to keep their targets then their parents are invited to school to discuss this problem.

The Community Taskforce

What is it?

The Community Taskforce is a lunchtime group that consists of a small number of children (between 3 and 7, depending on their specific needs) who work on a variety of projects during lunchtimes. The group may include:

● children beyond
● children who will be able to act as positive role models within the group by sharing their personal and social skills.

Why a Community Taskforce?

This group provides a way of addressing the needs of and supporting children in your school during playtimes. It will help you to implement your lunchtime/playtime and inclusion policies. Although the main focus is to help and empower the children beyond, the outcomes will have a positive effect on the emotional and physical wellbeing of the school's members as a whole.

Clearly there are funding implications involved in setting up a programme like this. Additional funds can be budgeted for, perhaps from the Special Educational Needs or the PSHE and Citizenship budget, and included in your school development plan. There are also external agencies you can apply to for funding to help your school promote this programme as part of your inclusion policy.

Setting up the Community Taskforce is a proactive way to help children learn skills and strategies that will enable them to become confident and valued members of the school community. As part of the group they will:

● develop personal and social skills
● experience positive interactions with their peers and adults
● learn practical skills
● develop emotionally healthy relationships
● learn team-building skills.

Who organises and runs the Community Taskforce?

The group may be set up by the head teacher, deputy head or SENCo, or by a member of staff with special responsibility for supporting children with emotional needs. Some schools recruit playleaders, youth or community workers, or parents to help support the group.

Members of staff are asked to be responsible for a 30-minute session one lunchtime a week. Staff members decide what activities the school is able to provide. The most effective and rewarding sessions are those in which the staff members have a particular interest, skill or enthusiasm that they are able to enthuse the children about.

The adult's role is to work with the children within a positive, creative and supportive atmosphere. The emphasis is on working with and empowering the children, rather than merely on encouraging them to help the adult. For example, 'We are working together to grow some plants' implies a feeling of shared responsibility. The children need to feel and believe that they are making a positive and valuable contribution to the project.

If any children beyond have additional help in class, it may be possible for you to negotiate additional support hours to help with this project. If this is not possible, the size of the group could be reduced to allow their specific needs to be met.

Examples of Taskforce projects

Furniture restoration

Staff and parents are asked to donate pieces of wooden furniture for restoration. This involves sanding, preparing and varnishing the furniture. It can then

be sold as part of your playtime fundraising programme.

Gardening club

This may involve growing plants from seeds and selling them to members of the school community, looking after the school plants, growing vegetables and herbs, or establishing a wildlife garden.

Drama club

In this club the group work on a piece of drama to share in an assembly.

Art and craft club

The group may work on their own individual projects for display in the school or make puppets for drama activities.

The self-esteem of all the group members, especially any children beyond, is boosted as they see the results of their efforts being appreciated by the school community.

Individual Playtime Programme

The Individual Playtime Programme is a structured programme that covers all playtimes for a 6–12 week period. The programme is similar to that of the Community Taskforce, but also includes a range of activities for morning and any afternoon playtimes. This programme provides additional support for any children beyond.

Children work with an adult in small groups of 3 to 4 children. A child beyond may choose someone to join them and the supervising adult also chooses one or two children. This helps to bring different children together to take part in the programme and enables the child beyond to learn from their peers.

The programme involves a range of activities and special responsibilities to help children beyond raise their self-esteem and develop their social skills.

Activities and responsibilities might include:

- playing chess, draughts or other board games
- using jigsaw puzzles or drawing and colouring
- lunchtime duties, such as scraping plates or wiping tables
- being part of the Community Taskforce
- taking part in a school drama or music club, which the supervising adult would also attend
- playing playground games in a small group with an adult.

Children beyond can go out to play for the last five minutes of each playtime and lunchtime. This can be extended as appropriate over a 6- to 12-week period. After this, children beyond can re-enter playtimes and lunchtimes with support and monitoring systems set in place – for example, the opportunity to participate in the Community Taskforce should they wish.

Example of a Individual Playtime Programme

Monday   Morning/afternoon playtime: playing chess, draughts or another board game
Lunchtime: drama club

Tuesday   Morning/afternoon playtime: listening to a story and acting it out with puppets
Lunchtime: lunch duties and drawing

Wednesday   Morning/afternoon playtime: making a collage
Lunchtime: lunch duties and drawing

Thursday   Morning/afternoon playtime: making a jigsaw puzzle
Lunchtime: Community Taskforce

Friday   Morning/afternoon playtime: watering plants
Lunchtime: doing special jobs for the head teacher

Playground Mentor or Guardian Angel

This is a particular type of Playground Friend (see chapter 3). A Playground Mentor or Guardian Angel is a Playground Friend who volunteers or is asked to support a child beyond for an agreed period of time. Both the child and the Playground Mentor meet regularly with the adult responsible for monitoring and supporting them to discuss any issues that may have arisen. The Playground Mentor's role may include:

● helping the child keep their playground targets
● supporting them as part of the Community Taskforce
● helping them with their Individual Playtime Programme
● being a friend to them
● being a good listener
● playing a game with them.

In one school where they have this system, a Playground Mentor chosen to work with a particular boy had a very calming effect on him. They both received merits at the end of playtime because the boy stayed out of trouble. Recognising and rewarding the Playground Friend is important for their self-esteem and sense of worth.

Some frequently asked questions about incentives and sanctions

Aren't supervisors too busy to be spending all their time writing out the mini-certificates?

Many children respond positively to the mini-certificates. If supervisors give out at least one a day it shouldn't take up too much time. The benefits are wonderful.

What about children who are just being good to get a mini-certificate?

They may start off like that, but positive recognition may encourage them to continue. If the teacher is busy, this may be one of the few times that a child is recognised for doing something positive, and it should be celebrated.

When we started, supervisors were enthusiastic, but after a few weeks I have noticed that some are not using the mini-certificates. What should I do?

Find out why. A reward and sanction system may not be needed in your playground because your other systems (zoning, Playground Friends) are well established and working well. Alternatively, supervisors may have other ideas they would like to try.

One of our supervisors is not using any of the incentives or sanctions, but complains about the behaviour in the playground. What should I do?

If the system agreed is not being used, it is very hard to follow up incidents. Supervisors must be part of the procedure; otherwise it will be ineffectual. Use a regular meeting to underline the reasons for and the value of incentives and sanctions.

Why should a child be able to get special treatment like sitting in the head teacher's office playing a game when everyone else is freezing outside in the cold?

If a child has reached this stage, all other options have been explored. The child may not have the social skills that are needed to play and interact positively with others. In fact, children don't like being separated from their friends, so their choices have also become limited. They do not have the freedom to go out and play.

What if the child refuses to go to the Community Taskforce?

The child's choices are very limited once you have got to this stage. It could be a choice between the Community Taskforce and lunchtime exclusion.

CREATING RULES, INCENTIVES AND SANCTIONS THAT WORK

Task	Have you:	Resources you may need	Person responsible/ monitored by	Estimated cost	Review date
Agree and display playground rules	• discussed the playtime rules with staff and supervisors? • had rules designed and printed for your school? • displayed rules for the playground?	• laminated playground rules			
Display safety rules	• discussed safety rules with staff and supervisors? • displayed safety rules in the playground next to the areas where the rules apply?	• safety rules			

Discuss incentives with supervisors	• decided which incentives to use:
	  ▶ 'I am pleased with you' mini-certificates
	  ▶ I am pleased with you' monitoring forms
	  ▶ lunchtime reward certificates
	  ▶ stickers
	  ▶ weekly raffle
	  ▶ lining-up merits.
		• monitoring forms
		• lunchtime reward certificates
		• 'I am pleased with you' mini-certificates
		• stickers
		• raffle tickets
		• prizes
		• merit certificates			

→

Task	Have you:	Resources you may need	Person responsible/ monitored by	Estimated cost	Review date
Link supervisors to a class/classes	• linked supervisors with a class/classes, to praise good individual/class behaviour? • asked supervisors to share good news and discuss any playground problems with their class/classes?	• class lists • timetable of class visits for the term			

Discuss sanctions with supervisors	• decided on sanctions to use?
	  ▲ 'I am disappointed' notelets
	  ▲ 'I am disappointed' monitoring forms
	  ▲ loss of Golden Time
	  ▲ loss of playtime
	  ▲ Incident forms
	  ▲ loss of football
	  ▲ lunchtime exclusion
		• 'I am disappointed' notelets
		• 'I am disappointed' monitoring forms
		• Incident forms			

Organise some Playground Friends to be Playground Mentors	• identified Playground Friends who want to support individual children in the playground? • approached a member of staff to monitor Playground Mentors? • identified training needs? • offered a training support programme?	• training and support for Playground Mentors			

→

CREATING RULES, INCENTIVES AND SANCTIONS THAT WORK

Task	Have you:	Resources you may need	Person responsible/ monitored by	Estimated cost	Review date
Set up a Community Taskforce	• identified supervisors or additional support to manage the group? • decided what activity you are going to set up? (furniture restoration, gardening project) • decided for how many days a week? • decided for how long each session will last?	• adult to supervise • old furniture • sandpaper • varnish • paintbrushes • plants, seeds • gardening tools, pots • earth, potting compost			
Help children beyond	• written playground targets and a weekly programme for children? • extended their free playtime gradually over a 6-week period?	• playground target card • Well Done certificate to be sent home			
Establish Individual Playtime Programme	• games for children to play? • a member of staff to supervise indoor activities? • a supervisor to support the child?	• games • playground target cards			

3 | *Playground Friends*

Who are the Playground Friends?

The Playground Friends are a group of children who apply for jobs to do during playtimes. These are caried out in the dining hall, in the playground, or inside during wet playtimes.

The Playground Friends:
★ help create a positive ethos in your school
★ show that they are committed to helping their peers
★ help raise the profile of the PSHE and Citizenship curriculum by demonstrating a caring attitude to other children
★ act as positive role models and teach values of caring and friendship.

Bringing out and putting away the equipment

It is very important to have a routine in which the equipment is taken and returned to the appropriate boxes at the end of playtime, otherwise it becomes lost or damaged.

Craze of the week

It is very helpful to have the craze of the week (see page 79) written up on a notice board so the children know which equipment they are to bring out. You might like to ask children to submit ideas for new crazes.

Teaching the traditional playground games

The Playground Friends will have their own copies of the games (see chapter 9), which they can refer to until they become familiar with the rhymes and rules.

If you are going to encourage children to play traditional playground games, then an adult needs to help to establish the daily routines; for example, in which part of the playground the games will be played. Once this has been established, the Playground Friends will become more confident to start them on their own.

Helping in the dining hall

There are many jobs the Playground Friends can do in the dining hall, such as scraping plates, wiping down tables and helping the younger children to cut up their food.

Helping lonely children make friends

By using the Friendship Stop, lonely children can signal to the Playground Friends that they need help (see page 81).

Sitting with unwell children

If a child is feeling unwell, a Playground Friend can sit with them and keep them company.

Other jobs

Ask the children in assembly or during the meetings what other jobs they would like the Playground Friends to do. Take ideas back to the school council and liaise with the supervisors about ways forward.

Why do you need Playground Friends?

The Playground Friends can help minimise many of the everyday issues that present themselves at playtimes and are typical of most schools, such as:

★ the child who is unhappy and lonely

★ the child who is afraid of being bullied and may wander around on their own or with the supervisors during lunchtimes

★ the child who finds it hard to make friends and bullies their way into other people's games

★ the parent who agonises about their child's welfare at playtimes

★ the teacher who has to spend time sorting out their class after a difficult playtime

★ the supervisor who doesn't have an opportunity to inform the teacher about any playtime problems

★ the supervisor who feels harassed because they are expected to do too much.

> *My best friend said she isn't my friend any more. I feel really sad, but at least I can go and talk to one of the Playground Friends and maybe play with them till my best friend wants to be my friend again.*
>
> *Year 3 child*

Why should a child be a Playground Friend?

Being a Playground Friend is a brilliant way of helping children to:

★ gain and build confidence and self-esteem

★ develop a genuine sense of responsibility by helping others improve playtimes

★ foster caring attitudes towards each other

★ grow emotionally when offered responsibility

★ realise that solutions to playtime problems often lie within themselves

★ learn moral values such as keeping to rules, turn-taking and sharing

★ evaluate and reflect on the effectiveness of rules and routines.

Getting started

There needs to be a member of the teaching staff and a member of the support staff involved in the development of the Playground Friends and the support of supervisors. These roles can be changed on a termly basis.

Before you instigate the Playground Friends, discuss the idea with your support staff and explain what they will do. This can minimise problems between staff and children whilst helping to set up the system effectively.

The person who is responsible for the scheme should meet at regular intervals with the supervisor in charge of the day-to-day management of the Playground Friends. This will allow them to address any issues that have arisen from the weekly meetings, and any other issues that have come to light. It will show strong support for the supervisor.

Informing your school community about the Playground Friends

Newsletter/information sheet

A school newsletter is a fantastic way of spreading good news and fresh initiatives. Children very often report back only snippets of information (if any at all!), and more often than not parents will hear the negative aspects of school life, and therefore only part of the picture. This can lead to parents having unnecessary concerns. For instance, in one school that was setting up a Playground Friends scheme, a parent complained that their child had to do jobs rather than playing. They didn't appreciate that their child had volunteered to join and thoroughly enjoyed it!

Use the newsletter to inform parents regularly about different aspects of your playtimes. Focus on one thing each time. Include direct quotes from children. They are much more likely to remember to give their parents the newsletter if there is something relevant to them in it.

> *Being a Playground Friend made Vanessa much more confident in the playground. She used to complain that she didn't have anyone to play with. But now she is helping other lonely children and at the same time she is making friends.*
>
> *Parent*

It is important to emphasise the fact that children have to apply to join and choose to do the job. No one is forced to be a Playground Friend!

Governors

Make sure that governors receive a copy of your newsletter. Governors need to know what happens at playtimes as they very often hear only about bullying or fundraising issues.

PTA

If your school has a PTA or other fundraising group, they may be keen to raise funds for various aspects of your playtimes.

Parents' notice board

Many schools have a parents' notice board. Use it to inform parents about playtimes:

★　Display photographs of the Playground Friends

★　Photocopy and enlarge quotes from the application forms showing why the children wanted to do the job

★　Display the newsletter in case it never gets home!

Assembly

Whole-school assemblies, at which as many teaching and support staff as possible are present, are an ideal place to introduce the idea of the Playground Friends. The head teacher, or another senior staff member, should take this assembly. Explain to the children that your school is going to have Playground Friends who will have special responsibilities in the playground to help children who want to learn new games, to look out for lonely children and to care for the equipment. Anyone interested will be able to apply for the job, which lasts half a term or a term. The Friends will have regular training and meetings to discuss playtime issues.

Posters with information about where to get the application forms can be displayed around the school (see page 178). These could be designed by the children.

Subsequent assemblies can focus on different aspects, such as:

★　demonstrating a new playground game

★　Playground Friends role-playing problems in the playground

★ zoning the playground

★ celebrating success and highlighting improvements that have been made.

Naming the Playground Friends scheme

An excellent way to engage children's interest and involve them from the start is to launch a competition to choose a name for your patrol of Playground Friends. One school introduced this idea during an assembly. The children had a week to write down their ideas and post them in a box. A name was later chosen by a small committee that included a selection of staff and children.

Names that have been adopted by schools include Friendship Squad, Playground Buddies and Guardian Angels as well as Playground Friends.

You may want to include your school's name in the title.

Applying for the job

Application forms (see page 179) should be available in each classroom, or in a place which is easily accessible for the children, during the first week of term. Children put their completed form in a box provided. Help should be offered to children who would like to apply but need assistance with filling in the form.

What children say about why they want to join

> *I would like to do this job because it helps children to play a nice game.*

> *Because I like helping people.*

> *So I can put the things out then people can play with them.*

> *I want this job because I want to help people and get a reward and I want to prove that I am confident.*

> *I want to show the children how to play a game in assembly and tell them why we want to be in the patrol. I used to be in the patrol, but I had a break and I've come back because people keep telling me I am really good at it!*

> *Because I want to make people happy, not sad.*

Interviews

Encourage children to apply within the first few days of term and then arrange a date to invite them for an interview with the adult who will be working with them. It may be difficult to interview children individually. Some schools interview them in small groups or pairs. Some schools invite people from local businesses to help with the interviews.

No one is refused a job. If you have too many children, you can put some on a waiting list. All children will receive a letter, either congratulating them and outlining the job or explaining that they are on a waiting list.

Ages

This depends on your school. Some schools invite all children interested to apply, especially if there are separate playgrounds and/or playtimes. Other schools limit application to Key Stage 2 classes or Year 6.

Uniform – spotting the Playground Friend

It's important that the Playground Friends are easy to identify when they are on duty. There are many types of uniform the children could wear. The most popular are caps. There are special Playground Friend caps supplied by Jenny Mosley (see page 199). Other options include tabards, badges and armbands.

Where to keep the uniform

Alternatives adopted by schools for Playground Friends include:

★ returning the uniform at the end of each day

★ keeping it in the Playground Friends' tray in their class and returning it at the end of each week

★   keeping it in the Playground Friends' tray and returning
     it at the end of half-term.

If you are going to use tabards, they will need to be washed on a fairly regular basis; otherwise they will start to look really grubby!

Day-to-day running of the system

Notice board

A notice board that is near the playground is a good place to put the rota and other information.

Rota

It is very important that children know the days or week they are on duty. Make a list of the jobs available. Have two teams, each team working every other week. You can have between 8 and 12 children in each team. Choose names for each team, or simply call them team A and B. Decide if each child is to work in a different area each week or to monitor the same area. You can also have a list of jobs that the children agree to do at the beginning of the week, or over a half-term.

The charts on pages 180 and 181 can be used in a variety of ways by the supervisor who is supporting the Playground Friends. They can:

★   fill in the names on the rota each day as a record of who was present
★   enlarge it to A3 and laminate it – each week the laminated rota is wiped
     clean and a new list is drawn up
★   enter lunchtime duties on the record sheet.

Rewards

In some schools children who are Playground Friends have a supply of mini-reward certificates that they can give out to other children (see page 182). They are encouraged not to give them to their best friend but to observe children who are really trying to be friendly or keep the playground rules. Each Playground Friend has between 10 and 15 mini-reward certificates, which should last them for the week they are on duty. Having a limited supply helps children to be selective. The giving of rewards is a great way to encourage peer praise and recognition.

> *I like to help the children and if they are lonely I get them someone to play with. I like giving out the mini-reward certificates because it makes me feel happy. We can make it better by showing other children respect. I don't like it when people don't respect you.*
>
> Playground Friend

Suggestion book

This is a book in which children can write ideas, suggestions or problems. It is placed somewhere that is easily accessible for the Playground Friends. The supervisors will read it and use it for discussion during meetings. Be careful that this book does not degenerate into a list of 'bad children'. We have seen such lists in a number of books. It may be helpful to have a page that is devoted to 'Children we need extra help with'.

Supporting the Playground Friends

Playground Friends meetings

The key supervisor, the teacher who is the lunchtime coordinator and the Playground Friends should have weekly 10–15-minute meetings. These are crucial to building an effective scheme and showing that you value what the children are doing. During this time you can:

★ check the rota and make sure everyone is clear about what they are doing for that week

★ say what the craze of the week is going to be

★ let the children raise any issues or concerns they have

★ look through the suggestion book together.

This is a short meeting so you may not be able to go into great depth, but you will become aware of the issues that you may need to tackle later. If there are management issues they need to be passed on to the head teacher, with a follow-up for the group at the next meeting, if appropriate.

Consulting the Playground Friends

Be sure to find out what the Playground Friends think about their role. You could use the questionnaire supplied on page 183 for this. Collect in the completed questionnaires and discuss the views of the Playground Friends at one of your meetings.

Celebrating and rewarding the Playground Friends

In assembly

All children who have completed their jobs receive a certificate and a small token (maybe a pencil or pen) as a thank you during a special assembly.

If there are children who would like to continue their involvement with the Playground Friends for another half-term, they could become Playground Mentors to new Friends. In the special assembly the names of the new Playground Mentors could be announced. There is often a rush of children ready to join the group as soon as the certificates and special thank yous are given out!

Other celebrations and incentives

There are many ways of showing your appreciation to the children. Some schools organise special outings for the Playground Friends or an end-of-term disco.

This could be extended so that every child who has been a Playground Friend is allowed to bring a guest (family member or school friend). Supervisors and the head teacher can also be invited. Drinks, food and music are provided to celebrate the children's achievements.

> We let the Friends have special privileges; for example, they can use the computers when they are not on duty. At the end of each year we take them all to the cinema or a show. Last year we took them to the theatre to see the musical 'Buddy' as a way of saying thank you.
>
> *Head teacher*

A school creates an attractive outdoor environment with Jenny Mosley's advice.

Regular Circle Time meetings for supervisors help to build team morale.

A group of children playing in the football zone.

Construction toys are popular at playtime.

Mixed key stage games help to promote positive relationships.

Golden Rules are the basis of peaceful playtimes.

A group of children enjoying a craze of the week.

A Playground Friend helping a lonely child at the Friendship Stop.

A group of children and a supervisor playing 'Duck, duck, goose'.

A group of children playing 'What's the time, Mr Wolf?' in the traditional games zone.

A member of the Community Taskforce prepares a bench for the playground.

Blackboards are a useful and enjoyable playtime resource.

Two children enjoying a lunchtime chess club.

Small games, such as dominoes, are enjoyable playtime activities.

A group of children playing an exciting game in the make-believe zone.

Large games, such as draughts, involve groups of children productively.

A group of children enjoying the gardening club.

Two children playing jacks during playtime.

A group of children playing in the parachute zone.

Some questions frequently asked when setting up the Playground Friends scheme

What if the supervisors don't think the scheme is a good idea?
As with any new initiative, it is vital to inform the people who will be directly involved, listen to their concerns and work together to address problems that occur.

What if too many children want to join?
You will find lots of children want to be Playground Friends. Decide how many you want on each rota and set up a waiting list.

Are applications forms available all the time?
This depends on how many children you have on your waiting list. If there are only a few names, you may want children to apply on an on-going basis. If you have lots on the list, you may want to leave some time before inviting fresh applications.

Is it really important to have regular meetings with the Playground Friends?
Definitely. One school we worked with stopped the meetings, lost most of their members and had to start again from the beginning. Children need to feel valued and to believe they make a difference in the playground.

What if members of the scheme fail to keep to the rota?
Is your rota easy to manage? If it is, ask the child if they have any problems they want to discuss. You may be able to sort this out, or they may not want to continue but don't want to say so. By talking to the children you may find a more effective way of managing the rota.

What can we do if other children are rude to the Playground Friends?
Playground Friends should always tell an adult if they are not happy with the way they have been spoken to. The head teacher can discuss behaviour in assembly. Use the training sessions to help children develop their assertiveness skills and to explore how to manage difficult situations.

What if children won't give the Friends the equipment back when the bell goes?
Assembly can be used to explain the playground rules. When the bell or whistle goes the equipment is handed to the Playground Friends. If not, the Playground Friends can ask for it again. A child who still refuses to cooperate is reported to a supervisor.

Can the Playground Friends give out sanctions when they are on duty?
Sanctions are not part of the job. They encourage some members to abuse their position by becoming heavy-handed, marching the children off to the supervisor and

dishing out punishments. If a child sees something that makes them concerned, they must tell a supervisor.

What happens if Playground Friends see other children fighting?

They should not get involved but find an adult and report the incident to them.

What should Playground Friends do if they see someone bullying, or are told about a bullying incident?

The role of the Playground Friends in the first instance is to be a good friend to whoever needs them. It is not their role to confront children involved in bullying or other conflict situations; these situations can be very complex and may need adult intervention. If the Playground Friends are concerned about something they have seen, or have been told by another child, they should report it to a supervisor who will deal with it in line with the school's positive behaviour and anti-bullying policies.

If your school has well-established Playground Friends, you may want to extend their duties to include peer mediation. This would require specific training that builds on the Playground Friends training described in chapter 4.

What happens if the Playground Friends are involved in fights?

If Playground Friends are involved in fights, or break the school's playtime rules, the playtime sanctions should apply to them. They will lose the privilege of being a Playground Friend and will have to return their uniform. They will however be able to apply again at a later date, having had time to reflect on their actions.

What if children with challenging behaviour want to be Playground Friends?

For these children being a Playground Friend can be used as an incentive to help improve their behaviour and give them a sense of responsibility. It should have a positive impact on their personal and social development. Such children can be invited to join the Playground Friends on a daily basis, which may be extended to a longer period if they continue to make progress with their behavioural targets. Participation as a Playground Friend can also be offered as a daily reward if classroom or playtime targets are achieved. For example, if a child's target is 'not to get involved in fights', aiming to be a Playground Friend may be a strategy to help them develop the skills needed to achieve this.

What if some of the Playground Friends are too bossy?

Often a gentle reminder about acceptable behaviour is enough. There are some special training sessions (see chapter 4) that will help the Playground Friends to practise appropriate responses to different scenarios.

What if no one wants to play the traditional games?

An adult should support the Playground Friends with the games initially. It may not be that children don't want to play, but that something new is happening and children will take time to get used to it. In one school we visited we found Playground Friends wandering around with their game card, saying 'No one wants to play this game.' Together, we found four children and started our game, 'I sent a letter'. By the end of the first playtime we had 15 children playing and singing along. One little girl was complaining that she hadn't had a turn yet, so I encouraged her to come back at lunchtime and continue.

What if the supervisors don't help the Playground Friends teach the games?

If your school has decided that they would like playground games as part of playtimes, then this has to be addressed as part of the school development plan – playtime policy being one of the key objectives.

Supervisors have a very difficult job in the playground and their main priority is to keep children safe. There are some supervisors whose main job is to police and sort out endless fights. The supervisor whose job it is to work in the traditional games zone to develop children's social skills and focus their energy on something constructive is far more productive.

What happens if a child doesn't want to be a Playground Friend any more?

No problem; there are probably children on the waiting list. Some schools require the child to write a letter of resignation if they want to leave.

Do children get a certificate if they resign before half-term?

That is up to you. If you are pleased with what they did, you may feel they should be rewarded.

If the children wear caps could they get head lice?

Only if they keep swapping them over while on duty. Writing a number in each cap enables the child to wear the same cap each day.

Whose job is it to keep the uniforms clean?

It is important that someone volunteers to wash the uniforms at the end of every half-term, either at home or using school facilities.

CASE STUDY

Inner-city primary school

Introduction

This is a case study of the first school we worked with to improve playtimes by introducing Playground Friends. It covers a 2-year period.

Playground Friends

We started the scheme in September 1998. During a meeting with the supervisors, we explained that the role of the Playground Friends was to teach games in the playground, manage zoned areas of the playground and befriend lonely children. We agreed our strategy for setting up the scheme and this was soon announced by the head teacher in assembly.

We ran a competition to find a name for the scheme. The children chose 'Playground Friends'.

Children interested in joining the Playground Friends filled in an application form. Our role was minimal at the beginning as the group was to be organised by the supervisors.

Seven children responded, mainly from Years 5 and 6. For the first few weeks we received positive feedback from the supervisors; the children were helping to take out and put away the equipment and teaching some games to other children. However, the quality of the children's participation diminished after this time. The supervisors felt disillusioned and they voiced their concerns, saying, 'It isn't working – the children are just not interested.'

Establishing the Playground Friends reinforced our belief that unless something works immediately people become cynical about change. We realised that we needed to boost everyone's morale and get the scheme back up and running before the supervisors could say it was a non-starter. We decided to take a more active role and prioritised this in January 1999.

We invited the children who had already worked on the scheme to a meeting and, feeling that we needed more children, we invited class teachers from Years 4, 5 and 6 to enlist more recruits. In all we relaunched with 19 children – 4 boys and 15 girls. The gender imbalance was not a concern at that time. The priority was to set the system up.

→

CASE STUDY

We had our first meeting in the staffroom at 1.30 one Thursday. This included all 19 children and 3 supervisors. We sat in a circle and watched a Jenny Mosley video about Playground Friends. The children were very excited and wanted to wear a cap, have a Friendship Stop and help out in the playground. We discussed the role of the patrol and the do's and don't's of the job. We felt there was slight resentment towards the scheme from the supervisors. It was important to begin to develop strong communication links between the children and the adults in the playground.

Discussion of a uniform dominated the rest of this hour-long session. Ideas included caps, sashes, badges and tabards. The supervisors, as well as the children, contributed ideas. Caps were the most popular amongst the children, partly because they saw them on the video and thought they looked 'cool'. One supervisor was against caps out of concern about the spreading of head lice. The last thing we wanted was for this initiative to be seen in a negative way, and we had already heard a parent say, 'I don't want my child in the group, they should be able to play at playtime.'

We took the decision that because the caps were so popular we would buy them and number each cap, which would then stay with a specific child until they left the group. Although the doubtful supervisor was not very keen, she felt that this was a fair compromise.

We were very excited and went out the same day to purchase the caps. We bought 20 in all and negotiated a reduced price for them. We bought four colours because there were not enough of one colour – we bought most of the stock in the shop! Had we foreseen the problems that lay ahead, we would have waited until we had enough of the same colour. We visited the classrooms from Year 4 upwards and gave children a choice of colour after we had numbered the caps. By the time we had reached Year 6 the 'best' colours had gone and what should have been an exciting time for the children turned into an anticlimax of comments like 'It's not fair!' and 'How come we were last to choose?' Some caps were too small, others too big, and they were not all washable. This all resulted in some of the children refusing to wear the caps because they were too tight and uncomfortable. In time, we made sure that we changed the caps for more suitable tabards that everyone was happy with.

We set up a rota, which gave the children two and a half days' duty per week. We started off by having weekly meetings for 30 minutes after lunchtime on

→

Thursdays. We had chosen this time as it was the most convenient for the supervisors. We were very aware that although teachers had agreed to their pupils' absence to attend the meetings, they were naturally not keen for the children to be out of the class for long. Over the first few weeks the meeting was done in a Circle Time style with clear ground rules.

When asked what they liked about their job, their comments included, 'I like helping the children' and 'I like children.' One girl said it helped her stay out of trouble. This was a girl who was constantly in trouble in class and had a very short concentration span. In the meetings she was able to follow the ground rules and participate in the discussion. We felt she had developed a sense of belonging in the group and we took note when she said 'My sister [who was in year 1] didn't have any friends, but I found her some and now she isn't lonely any more.' The Playground Friends developed good links with the supervisors and, when the scheme was working, it worked well. The children became allies with the supervisors rather than rebels, especially the Year 6's, who may go off the rails during their last term because of their imminent departure from the school.

Many children thrived on the responsibility that the job gave them and took pride in what they did, especially befriending lonely children. One boy said, 'I found seven of them today.' At first they were so enthusiastic about this part of the job that any child who stood still would be approached and paired off with someone. Fortunately this slowed down after a while!

There were still problems to resolve; for example, children were not keeping to the rota. There were many reasons for this: they were fed up, interest had diminished, it wasn't fun any more, there was no clear job description, they wanted to play with their friends, other children told them to get lost and children were not listening to them. This gave some of them an insight into the difficult job that the supervisors have. They commented on how rude some of the children were and how little attention they paid.

We used the Circle Time session to address some of these issues, to look at possible strategies and to report back their experiences. Over a few weeks some improvements were reported. However, it was important for the children to develop an understanding that change can be a long process which involves hard work and commitment.

The weekly meetings were becoming a problem because the 30-minute sessions were going on for at least 45 minutes by the time supervisors came in and we got

→

CASE STUDY

started. So we changed the meetings to fortnightly, lasting for from 45 minutes to an hour. This gave us opportunities to tackle at least one concern each time as well as to look at the positive things that were happening.

The drinking fountains were one of the problems the group worked on. As soon as the bell went at the end of playtime, a group of children would go over to the water fountains and not leave until they got a drink of water. When they were asked by the Friends to leave, they refused and were sometimes rude to them. This situation was found to be partly a management issue as out of the four drinking fountains only one was in working order. However, in spite of this a supervisor came up with a solution, which was that a bell was rung by one of the Playground Friends a few minutes before each playtime was over. That gave the children time to queue up for a drink.

Over the first two terms we had three children in the group at our lowest point. One child in particular stayed with us and did his very best at all times. He was average in class but shone in the playground. We gave him a special thank you in our end-of-term assembly, where all Playground Friends were given a certificate and a pencil.

Another notable Playground Friend was a girl from one of the group of travellers in the school. The children of travellers make up 10% of the school population and many of them have problems integrating with the rest of the children. This girl not only did the job of being a Playground Friend extremely well, but her status rose in the playground, especially with the young children whom she befriended and helped. She also made suggestions about how we could improve things in the playground.

Playground Friends have access to a reward system comprising slips of paper that praise positive behaviours in the playground and a notebook that is used to write down issues or observations. These can be discussed during the Playground Friends meetings.

Conclusion

September 2000

Two years on we found many of the systems we had in place were not being sustained because there was no key person who was prepared to take responsibility for helping the Playground Friends become established.

→

CASE STUDY

Two of our supervisors were asked to take responsibility for working with a team every other week to see if this would help. We have two teams of about ten children who are Playground Friends every other week. Each team is supervised by one of the two supervisors.

Every Monday morning the team on duty for that week has a 15-minute meeting with their supervisor. This takes place during assembly.

> *I'm getting quite excited about my team. I'm going to get a little book from the pound shop and put the names of the children in my team in it. When I am on duty I will wear a red band on the Monday so my team will know it's our week. If they are not on duty I'll remind them. They might be having a bad day, we all do sometimes, but as long as they tell me they need a break, that's fine with me.*
>
> *Supervisor*

The children discuss which jobs they would like to do and the supervisor marks that on a rota and pins it up on the notice board. The meetings are a good opportunity to discuss issues the children or supervisor have.

Some children drop out but there are always children who are ready to take their place.

> *It really makes a difference having a team each and having that few minutes on a Monday to talk to the children. When they wear their tabards, I can see immediately who is on duty and it was really helpful the other day when we were in the dining hall and I needed some help. I just looked to see who was wearing their tabard and called out their names and they came over right away, I think I'm going to enjoy this.*
>
> *Supervisor*

> *I like my team and there are so many children who want to join. I think we are really getting it sorted.*
>
> *Supervisor*

CASE STUDY

The Playground Friends have become an important part of playtimes. The most effective part is the supervisors helping the group in the regular meetings. They help them to manage difficult situations, like rudeness from the other children.

We have learned the most important thing is that everyone works together and finds solutions to the problems. This shows that we believe in the Playground Friends and believe that they are making a difference to children in the playground. We feel very proud of the children. The two supervisors have worked really hard with them and this is shown by the children's commitment to the group.

PLAYGROUND FRIENDS

Task	Have you:	Resources you may need	Person responsible/ monitored by	Estimated cost	Review date
Setting up your Playground Friends scheme	• organised a meeting with supervisors? • identified a supervisor who will work with and support the Playground Friends? • selected a senior member of staff with an interest in playtimes who will support the supervisor? • had an assembly to tell the children and staff what the Playground Friends do and how they can join? • explained why you are going to introduce the Playground Friends in your school? • put posters around the school advertising the job and saying where to get the application form? • outlined the jobs available? • organised a competition to choose a name for the Playground Friends? • decided how long the job is for? • decided what age groups you will focus on? • discussed the rewards and privileges? • decided when you can interview the children and who will do it? • sent letters to the children who have been interviewed? • started a waiting list if there are too many children?	• application forms • folder • acceptance letters • posters			

→

Task	Have you:	Resources you may need	Person responsible/ monitored by	Estimated cost	Review date
Get a uniform	• decided what the group will wear? • decided where it will be kept? • decided who will keep it clean?	• caps • tabards • badges • bands			
Establish the day-to-day running of the Playground Friends	• allotted a space on the notice board near the playground? • taken photographs of the teams? • written up a rota? • created and named two teams? • alternated the teams week by week? • written a list of jobs they can do each day? • organised a good supply of mini-reward certificates for the Playground Friends to give out? • found a place to keep the suggestion book? • written up what the craze of the week is? • chosen a supervisor to help teach the craze of the week? • chosen a supervisor to help teach the traditional playground games?	• notice board • rota • camera • list of jobs • reward slips • suggestion book • laminated game cards • craze of the week equip-ment • playground games booklets			
Supporting the Playground Friends	• organised a weekly 10–15-minute meeting with the Playground Friends on duty and the supervisor, to discuss any issues and feedback positive experiences?	• a room to meet in			

→

PLAYGROUND FRIENDS

Task	Have you:	Resources you may need	Person responsible/ monitored by	Estimated cost	Review date
Informing parents and the wider community	• written a piece in your school newsletter about the Playground Friends? • put a notice up on the parents' notice board? • introduced a special playground newsletter telling parents about the Playground Friends? • agreed to do a talk at a governors' meeting? • used quotes from the application forms as a display, to show why children want to be Playground Friends? • asked the PTA to raise funds for a uniform?	• parents' notice board • playground newsletter • quotes to go in the display			
Celebrate and reward the Playground Friends	• organised a special assembly to thank the children every half-term? • thought about an event for the Playground Friends to which they can each invite one guest? • organised an outing? • invited supervisors and the head teacher to join in with these events?	• certificates • gifts • food and drink • music			

4 | *Meetings and training sessions for the Playground Friends*

The training sessions

When children first join the Playground Friends they are enthusiastic and eager to do the job. If they do not have basic social skills to help them, however, they may feel disheartened when other children are rude to them, or they may be overbearing towards others.

Spending time developing communication and cooperation skills will build the children's confidence and demonstrate how their behaviour can have a positive or negative impact on others.

> *In the Playground Friends I feel OK, but sometimes when I say to people 'Do you want a friend?', they say 'Shut up and go away.'*
>
> Playground Friend

The training sessions have been developed to enable children to:

▶ develop an understanding about rules, roles and responsibilities

▶ learn to respect each other

▶ identify their own skills and qualities

▶ develop skills to help them communicate and cooperate effectively

▶ use assertive statements to express how they feel

▶ develop effective strategies to understand and manage their anger

▶ develop skills needed for problem-solving.

Delivering the sessions

The five sessions can be used as they are, or you can add a quick warm-up game at the beginning. Establish the ground rules for your sessions, such as 'No put-downs', 'We listen carefully to each other'. End the session with a playground game from chapter 9. It is a good idea to find out what is going well and celebrate the success stories children have to share.

To help identify other training needs, ask for suggestions and use them to plan future sessions.

Playground Friends' booklet

The booklet (see pages 184–187) has been designed to be filled in during the sessions. It can be kept by the children to refer to and add to as part of a continuing learning programme.

When should training take place?

Ideally the training sessions should take place within the first few weeks of children first joining the Playground Friends. Allow three to four hours in total to cover the five sessions. Your school needs to decide on the best time to do them.

Who should deliver the training sessions?

The person who will take responsibility for the ongoing support of the Playground Friends should deliver the training. This will vary from school to school and could be the head teacher, the deputy or the SENCo. A supervisor should, if possible, take part in the training sessions too. This would be a huge asset to the bonding of the group and help to develop mutual respect. The supervisor develops an understanding of and empathy for the role of Playground Friends and discernment of the skills they need. The Playground Friends learn to appreciate the point of view of support staff.

Children who join after the training sessions

One way of addressing the needs of those who join after the initial training is for a confident member of the Playground Friends to shadow the new member and be their mentor for a short period of time, modelling the behaviour that is expected of them. The new Friend should be given a copy of the booklet and if possible spend time with their mentor for help with the activities.

The booklet helps me to think about different things and try out some of the ideas we talked about.

Playground Friend

A last word

Establishing the training at an early stage is time consuming and you may be tempted to skip it. The training, however, will contribute to the ethos in your school community and help children to develop into responsible individuals with a sense of empathy, care and respect for their peers and adults.

Training session 1

Aim: to familiarise the Playground Friends with their rules, routines and responsibilities.

- **Round:** I want to be a Playground Friend because ...

- **Group rules**

Why do we need rules? We need to decide together on some rules for our scheme. Write them down.

Examples:
We help and support each other
We keep to the rota when we are on duty
We call an adult if we see a fight
We don't hand out sanctions.

- **Playground rules and safety routines**

What are the playground rules in our school?
Why is it important to keep to the rules?
What happens if children break the rules?
What happens if you break the playground rules? (for example, a written warning issued and then loss of the privilege of being a Playground Friend)
What are the safety routines in your school? (for example, keep off the grass, don't climb on the walls)

- **Responsibilities**

Ask children to tell you all the duties they think are part of their job. Write them on a flipchart and discuss. Delete the ones that don't apply.
Ask them about their responsibilities to their job. (for example, take my job seriously, do my best, support the others in my group)

- **Making a difference**

Brainstorm the following questions and use a flipchart to record the answers.

What makes a good playtime? (being with friends, feeling happy, playing games)
What makes a bad playtime? (feeling lonely or left out, fighting, nothing to do)
Can you think of anything you could do to help children have a good playtime? (teach games, be kind, get games out to play)

- **Closing round:** One thing I can do is .../One quality I bring ...

Training session 2

Aim: to agree on the practical aspects of the daily system of the Playground Friends.

- **Routine**

Discuss the following with the group:

▶ How the rota will work, where it will be pinned up and how the jobs will be shared.

▶ What the uniform is going to be and where it will be kept.

▶ Where the equipment will be kept and who will collect it.

▶ A list of games for the craze of the week.

▶ When the weekly/fortnightly meetings will be held.

▶ Who is responsible for supporting the group.

- **Questions**

Use these as starting points for discussions:

What if ...

you see someone wandering around on their own?

you think someone is being bullied?

children are rude to you?

children are not looking after the playground equipment?

- **Closing round:** I am looking forward to ...

Training session 3

Aim: to identify skills and qualities needed to communicate and cooperate effectively with others.

- **Role play**

Ask two Friends to role-play the following scenario. The rest watch carefully and see what happens.

The first child is sitting on a bench, looking sad. The second is a Playground Friend. The Playground Friend goes over to the child and says and does things to make the child feel uncomfortable (for example, shouting at the child, being really noisy, giving them orders, laughing at them or pulling them up).

- **Discussion**

Use a flipchart to write down the responses:

First ask the children in the role play how they felt, then ask all the children to tell you what they saw and heard.

Include the following questions:

How was the Playground Friend standing?
How close were they?
What was the tone of their voice?
How did they speak?
What was the expression on their face?

Repeat the exercise either with the same or different children and ask them to do things that make the child feel comfortable and safe. They can include any of the following: being friendly, speaking in a soft voice, sitting next to them, listening to what they say, asking them how they feel, repeating what the child said to show that they have been listened to.

Use a flipchart to write down their responses:

First ask the children in the role play how they felt, then ask all the children to tell you what they saw and heard.

- **Communication**

Ask the children to make a list of all the qualities and skills needed to communicate and cooperate effectively and write them on the flipchart.

What sort of questions could you ask a child who may be lonely?

Possible answers include:

> What's your name?
>
> What class are you in?
>
> Have you got any brothers or sisters?
>
> Have you got any friends in school today?
>
> What games do you like playing?

- **Role play**

Ask children for examples of how they can help someone find a friend at playtime and how to ask a group if they can join in with their game. Role-play the situations using the qualities and skills they have learned.

- **Closing round:** One thing I am good at .../One thing I need to work on ... /One thing I have learnt from this session ...

Training session 4

Aim: to practise using 'I' statements to help you to be assertive, to say how you feel and to get what you want without being aggressive or blaming the other person.

- **Role play**

Ask volunteers to act out the following scenario.

The whistle has gone for the end of playtime. Jack won't give the equipment back to the Playground Friend. The Playground Friend reacts angrily.

PLAYGROUND FRIEND:	Can I have the skipping rope back?
JACK:	I'm playing with it.
PLAYGROUND FRIEND:	Didn't you hear the whistle for the end of playtime? Give it to me!
JACK:	Why should I?
PLAYGROUND FRIEND:	You never listen, do you? I'm going to tell the supervisor so they can tell you off.
JACK:	**I** want to put it back.
PLAYGROUND FRIEND:	It's **my** job to put it back.

Ask the children doing the role play how it felt.
Ask everyone what made the problem worse. Did anything make it better?

Repeat the role play, this time using 'I' statements, the Playground Friend remaining calm.

PLAYGROUND FRIEND:	Can I have the skipping rope, please?
JACK:	I'm playing with it.
PLAYGROUND FRIEND:	**I feel** really annoyed because I asked for the skipping rope back and you were rude to me.
JACK:	Why should I give it back?
PLAYGROUND FRIEND:	**Because** the whistle has gone and it's my job to collect them. **I want** you to give it to me straightaway next time.
JACK:	OK.

Ask the children doing the role play how it felt.

Ask everyone what the difference was between the two scenarios (one sounded aggressive, the other assertive, the children said clearly how they felt).

Emphasise that using 'I' statements won't always work, but in the role play the Playground Friend has spoken to the other person with respect and has been able to express how they felt and what they wanted to happen.

- **Closing round:** One thing I have learnt is …

Training session 5

Aim: to understand and manage anger.

- **Talking about anger**

Explore and build a word bank of different emotions by asking children how they would feel if:

▶   they had lots of presents for their birthday

▶   their pet rabbit died

▶   they were blamed for something they didn't do

▶   their best friend had an argument with them.

Write the words on a flipchart.

At this point stress that anger is a powerful emotion and it's OK to feel angry, but you need to find safe ways of managing your angry feelings without hurting yourself, other people or property.

Using the flipchart, ask children to make a list of things that make them angry. Remember not to mention anyone's name. Ask them why these things make them angry.

What happens to their body when they are angry? (fists clenched, red face, heart pounding, foot stomping, eyes bulging)

How do they behave when they are angry? (kick, fight, punch, refuse to talk, cry)

- **Managing anger**

Can you think of safe ways to manage your angry feelings without hurting yourself, other people or property?

Suggestions:

Find a quiet place to calm down

Run around the playground

Count to 10

Have time out

Find someone to talk to

Read a book

Write down your feelings

Calm down before you talk about it

Speak to a good friend.

Can you think of what you could say to someone to help them calm down in the playground?

- **Closing round:** When I feel angry I will try ...

MEETINGS AND TRAINING SESSIONS FOR THE PLAYGROUND FRIENDS

Task	Have you:	Resources you may need	Person responsible/ monitored by	Estimated cost	Review date
Timetable and deliver the training sessions	• identified someone to deliver the training sessions and take responsibility for supporting the Playground Friends and supervisor? • timetabled the training sessions? • invited a supervisor to take part in the training sessions?	• flipchart • marker pens • budget for supervisor to attend			
Give the Playground Friends their own booklet	• used the booklet as part of the training sessions? • discussed how to fill it in?	• copies of the Playground Friends' booklet			
Consider children who join after the training sessions	• thought about children being mentors to help the children who have missed out on the training? • made sure they have a booklet, and if possible that their mentor helps them to fill it in?				

5 | *Effective Circle Time meetings for lunchtime staff*

Over the past ten years, we have facilitated more than 300 Circle Time sessions with lunchtime staff. In our experience people are open and honest when they feel they are in a safe and trusting environment in which their views and feelings are recognised and valued without being criticised. Initially some members of staff feel strange sitting in a circle because it isn't what they are used to. Sometimes in a classroom there are children sitting at the back of the class who don't want to be seen. There have been occasions rather like this when we have waited for someone to join the circle and stop sitting at the table. It is important to explain that the circle gives a sense of togetherness and equality. It has a democratic approach that enables everyone to be seen.

The group agreement, which sets out the rules, is made and agreed by the group in your first session. It is tempting to miss out the warm-up games because of lack of time, but it is very often these games that loosen people up. By laughing and sharing feelings we become able to empathise with and understand each other better.

Looking back on the very first meeting, we were enthusiastic and somewhat naïve. Sure that we were going to be welcomed with open arms on account of our fantastic ideas and strategies, we were taken aback when people were negative about our suggestions for improvement. That was the problem – they were *our* suggestions. They were from the Quality Circle Time model. The problem was that we were so keen to get started that we were thinking too much about where we were going and too little about how we, as a group, were going to get there.

> *When support staff feel valued and respected they will be more able to take on the challenge of changing systems and changing their own attitudes and behaviour.*
>
> Head teacher

The following guidelines are intended to help you structure your sessions with clear ground rules and a definite focus. Regular meetings with your supervisors are crucial to the ongoing maintenance, review and improvement of your lunchtime system.

Guidelines for meetings

Your role

Your role should be to act as a facilitator, allowing the views and issues to be debated, guiding the group and informing where appropriate. When the meetings become established a supervisor may like to take on the facilitator's role.

Duration of meetings

Ideally the meetings should last for an hour. This will allow some of the issues to be discussed in depth and give everyone an opportunity to contribute.

The meeting itself

Getting started

Arrange some chairs in a circle beforehand. Start off your session with some refreshments. It is very important to agree a set of rules in your first meeting that will help to create a safe environment for the group, encouraging members to participate.

Ask the group to decide on the rules, which might include:

- no put-downs
- listen to each other
- respect what others say, even if you don't agree
- no moans without a suggestion for change.

Your first meeting may feel quite negative. This may be the first time your supervisors have been invited to a meeting and asked for their views. It is important that individuals are allowed to express their feelings. Once negative feelings have been addressed, if possible move on. When you do focus on problems, don't allow the session to be dominated by them. Try to find a way to bring the discussion back to finding solutions to the problems. Ask people to work in pairs, sharing one thing they like and one they dislike about their job. This will encourage the group members to talk and listen to each other.

Rounds

In a round people speak in turn, when a speaking object (often a decorative egg or shell) is handed to them.

We have found that when we introduce the egg in the round group members feel a little odd and self-conscious, but in a short time they come to see this as a very important and special part of the meeting. There have been many times when someone has been interrupted in mid-sentence by the words, 'Excuse me, I've got the egg, thank you!' There are many ways of introducing the speaking object and you may want to end with it, passing it round to enable everyone to evaluate the session, or to complete a specific statement such as 'One thing I found useful today was ... '.

By the second meeting you can help the group feel more at ease by asking them to work on an activity in pairs, feeding back what the other person has said to the whole group. People usually find it easier to talk about their partner than about themselves and this may be the first time they have been involved in a meeting where they have been asked for their opinions and views. When the person speaking has finished, they should ask their partner if they left anything out.

Open forum

This is the part that helps to focus and develop strategies for improving your playtimes. On pages 69–76 we have provided outlines of meetings, covering ideas for delivering different aspects of the playtime improvement in your school. As an introduction you may give an overview of the different areas and then focus on one in more depth. If there are too many issues, they become diluted and you will find that you do not have time to address any of them properly. You may have already decided with your senior staff which one to start with, or you may want your support staff to identify one they would like to work on, such as:

- zoned activity areas
- Playground Friends
- rewards and sanctions
- links with teaching staff
- guidelines for good relationships
- wet playtimes
- the dining hall.

As the group becomes accustomed to meeting regularly, they will begin to build a team spirit. When you have identified an area to work on, ask for suggestions, using the phrases:

Would it help if ...

Would it help to know ...

At first, group members may find this strange, but it helps to keep people's minds focused on finding a solution rather than becoming fixed on how bad the problem is or going off at a tangent. Remember:

- focus on the problem
- brainstorm ideas
- choose and agree one or two ideas to try.

There is a much better chance of the ideas working if the group have suggested them.

Set the date for the next meeting

It is very important to set the date for the following meeting; it can easily be forgotten.

Closing the meeting positively

End with a round such as: One thing I will take away from today's session .../One thing I've learnt today ...

Minutes of meetings and reviews

Writing up the minutes and distributing them helps to enhance the importance of the meetings. It also enables you to highlight the areas you have targeted. Always review progress, problems and successes at subsequent meetings. That enables you to show that the meetings can have a positive effect, changing and improving situations.

Meeting with supervisors:
Guidelines for good relationships with children

You will need: photocopies of the guidelines for good relationships between children and lunchtime supervisors (see pages 70–71).

- Ask participants to work in pairs. Give each pair a copy of the handout and allocate two or three sections to each pair, asking them to discuss and decide whether they agree with the statements, supporting their views with some examples. *Duration, 5 minutes*

- Back in the main group, ask each pair to read out their sections and any examples they may have. Ask the whole group if they would like to add anything before moving on to the next pair.

- When you have completed the activity the group agrees the sections they will include as part of your school guidelines, if necessary adapting some so that you can all agree on them. *Duration, 30 minutes*

- Have a round using the statements:
  One thing I do well …
  I need to try harder at …

  This encourages the supervisors to share publicly their strengths and areas they need to improve on. Ask how they think they will achieve the latter. *Duration, 5 minutes*

- Discuss what training the group would like to help them with the guidelines. *Duration, 15 minutes*

Guidelines for good relationships between children and lunchtime supervisors

1   Treat all children fairly and equally
It's all too easy to jump to wrong conclusions about a situation. The children must be given an opportunity to explain their behaviour. Don't act on hearsay, only act on what you are sure you saw.

2   Be friendly and approachable
Children need to see you as someone who is open and ready to listen to them. A cold or distant manner will stop them from approaching you.

3   Give gentle reminders
Children often simply forget some rules; for example, not running in the dining hall. A gentle reminder may be all that is needed.

4   Stay calm
Try to stay calm at all times. This will help you to remain in authority and be effective. If you shout or boss the children about they may think you're losing control.

5   Smile
Try to remember to smile at the children. They will then see you as someone warm and friendly.

6   Try to chat
Be willing to chat to the children about their news, interests and activities.

7   Give praise
Praise is more effective than criticism, so try to praise frequently.

8   Give incentives
Use any special stickers or incentives that the school has.

9   Be polite
Set a good example to the children by speaking politely to them.

10   Avoid getting into a confrontation

Don't argue with a child; that undermines your authority. Repeat your request calmly, then use your sanctions system. Don't become involved in slanging matches with a child. If you have to deal with bad behaviour, take the child/children to one side, away from others who might encourage them.

11   Help a child 'back out' of an awkward situation

If a child is deliberately rude, ask them politely to repeat what they said. This allows the child to retract the statement or apologise. Accept any apology graciously and don't reprimand them further. Don't leave the child with no way out. If the child feels cornered there is a danger of confrontation.

12   Don't shout

Avoid shouting at all times. Shouting at children can have a negative effect on their behaviour and make some children very defensive. It will make your job much more difficult. If the noise level is high ask the head teacher if there are other ways in which you can gain silence.

13   Learn from the class teacher

Speak to, observe and learn from the class teacher and other support staff who use other ways than shouting to achieve quiet.

14   Don't use sarcasm

Don't belittle children by using sarcasm – this leads to resentment.

15   Don't use labels

Don't give children negative labels such as 'naughty', 'rude' or 'stupid'. Tell the child their behaviour is unacceptable.

16   Watch out for loners

Watch out for lonely or isolated children. Talk to them and try to involve them in games with other children.

17   Personal remarks

Don't make a negative personal remark to a child. You will never make a relationship with that child if you do.

Meeting with supervisors: Divide the playground into zoned activity areas (see chapter 6)

You will need: outline of your playground on a sheet of A3 paper.

● Depending on how many people attend the meeting, work in one group or a number of smaller groups. Give each group an outline map of your playground and ask them to write on it what each area is used for at present. *Duration, 15 minutes*

Discuss the following areas, using a flipchart to record comments:

● the zoning idea

● how many zones to start with

● ideas about how to mark out the zones (paint, cones, chalk, small maps on the wall)

● what equipment and resources are required (hoops, skipping ropes) and where they will be stored

● who will manage the zones and how they will do this – you may like to start with three zones, such as:

    quiet zone

    football zone

    craze of the week zone (start with two or three crazes that you can alternate on a weekly basis).

As the zones develop you might like to add one or two of the following:

● dressing-up zone

● traditional games zone

● music and dance zone

● construction zone. *Duration, 45 minutes*

Meeting with supervisors: Introducing the Playground Friends (see chapter 3)

You will need: sample of the application form, a flipchart and pens, and video of Playground Friends.

● Give an outline of what the Playground Friends are.

Duration, 10–15 minutes

● Discuss how the supervisors and Playground Friends can support each other. *Duration, 20 minutes*

● Either work as a whole group or split into smaller groups and discuss the following:

What do you think of this idea?

What advantages would it bring to our school?

Can you see any disadvantages? How could we address these?

Is this something our school can take on board?

● Record ideas on the flipchart. *Duration, 30 minutes*

Meeting with supervisors: Develop your rules, rewards and sanctions (see chapter 2)

You will need: flipchart and pens.

- As a whole group discuss what the playtime/lunchtime rules are in your school.

  Write them on the flipchart, using positive statements where possible; for example:

  Do be gentle, don't hurt people   *Duration, 15 minutes*

- Do they need to be displayed?   *Duration, 5 minutes*

- In pairs discuss what rewards and sanctions you have during playtimes/lunchtimes.   *Duration, 5 minutes*

- In a group use the flipchart to make a list of them.
  Which of these work well?
  Which need to be improved?   *Duration, 10 minutes*

- Discuss the sanctions used in your school at present.
  What happens if children consistently break the rules?
  Is your sanction system effective?   *Duration, 10 minutes*

- Give an overview of the section on rewards and sanctions and ask for comments.
  Agree to try something from chapter 2.   *Duration, 10 minutes*

- Discuss the idea of the Community Taskforce and ask for ideas from the group about how it could benefit the school.   *Duration, 10 minutes*

Meeting with supervisors:
Wet playtimes (see chapter 8)

You will need: flipchart and pens.

- In pairs discuss the concerns and issues you have about wet playtimes. Use the flipchart and make a list.   *Duration, 10 minutes*

- As a group discuss which parts of wet playtimes work well.
  Make a list of resources you have for wet playtimes.
  Make a list of resources you would like. Could you use any of the playground equipment?   *Duration, 20 minutes*

- Highlight two concerns about wet playtimes that they would like to improve.   *Duration, 5 minutes*

- Discuss the ideas in chapter 8 and consider how they can be implemented.
                                                   Duration, 20 minutes

Meeting with supervisors:
Lunchtime routines (see chapter 7)

You will need: photocopies of the lunchtime audit questionnaire (see page 188), a flipchart and pens.

- Divide the meeting into two groups. Give each group a questionnaire and ask them to discuss the questions.   *Duration, 15 minutes*

- Ask each group to share their findings.   *Duration, 20 minutes*

- Discuss the ideas from chapter 7 and how they could implement two of them.   *Duration, 15 minutes*

Meeting with supervisors: Links with teachers

You will need: flipchart and pens.

- Divide the group into pairs and ask them to discuss how they communicate with teachers about playtimes and lunchtimes.   *Duration, 10 minutes*

- Feed back to the main group.

  Discuss what the issues are that prevent them from communicating with teaching staff.

  Write the issues on the flipchart.

  Can you think of any ways of helping communication?

  Duration, 10 minutes

- Discuss the ideas in the first chapter of this book.

  Choose one to try and review at the next meeting.

  Duration, 30 minutes

EFFECTIVE CIRCLE TIME MEETINGS FOR LUNCHTIME STAFF

Task	Have you:	Resources you may need	Person responsible/ monitored by	Estimated cost	Review date
Develop effective training sessions	<ul><li>organised training sessions for supervisors?</li><li>identified someone who will deliver the training sessions?</li><li>decided where the sessions will take place?</li><li>decided the time the sessions will take place?</li><li>provided refreshments?</li><li>budgeted for the training sessions?</li></ul>	<ul><li>refreshments</li><li>a room to meet in</li><li>a speaking object such as a decorated egg</li><li>flipchart</li><li>pens</li><li>paper</li></ul>			

6 | *Zoning the playground*

Bored or bad behaviour? Create zoned playgrounds and find out!

Many playground issues – such as fighting, bullying and loneliness – stem from children being bored and lacking the skills they need to make friends, cooperate, take turns and interact with each other. Zoning is simply a way of dividing your playground into specific activity areas, making opportunities to help children channel their energies and use their time in imaginative and creative ways. This in turn helps you to make better use of your space and enables the playground to be shared more fairly, preventing bigger games like football dominating.

How to zone

To create clear boundaries between each zone you can use paint, cones, chalk, trees, shrubs or benches.

Looking after your equipment

Equipment should be kept in a secure place only accessible to the supervisors and Playground Friends. It is cost effective to invest in a lockable shed or large cupboard to keep your equipment safe. Due to wear and tear, equipment will need replacing regularly.

> *We kept our playground equipment in a box just outside a classroom in a hut. Children coming out of the class were helping themselves and we ended up with very little. Now the Playground Friends organise and look after the equipment.*
>
> *Supervisor*

Introducing zoned areas

Discussion with the supervisors about the zoning is crucial. It will encourage participation and provide them with opportunities to make positive contributions and air concerns. To help decide which zones to introduce, it is a good idea to find out how the space is currently used. One way to do this is to draw a map of the playground and ask the supervisors and children to write or draw what happens in the different parts. You may find a difference between how staff and children perceive the uses of these areas. For example, the quiet area with lovely plants and shrubs may not be the pleasant 'chat with your friends' space, but a blind spot where bullying occurs.

A discussion with supervisors and a small group of children from the Playground Friends, school council or class representatives can be held to decide where to mark the proposed zones on a map of the playground.

Start off gradually, introducing no more than three zones. These might be football, craze of the week and traditional playground game zones. Each of these requires one type of equipment only, which makes the zones easier to manage. When these zoned areas have become established, you may want to introduce additional ones.

Do experiment to find out what works for your school.

Ideas for zoned activity areas

The following ideas have been tried and tested in many schools to improve the quality of playtimes.

Craze of the week

The craze of the week has been created to enable children to develop the ability to use equipment appropriately, as well as the skills needed to cooperate and take turns. One type of equipment is brought out to play every day for a week; for example, hula hoops, skipping ropes, french skipping, bats and balls or bean bags. You need to have a large amount of each so that anyone who wants to play is able to – for example, 40 skipping ropes, or 40 sets of bats and balls. Having one type of equipment out each week not only adds excitement but, through play, helps motivate the children to develop and expand their skills.

The crazes can be explained and demonstrated by members of the Playground Friends during special assemblies on playtimes.

Starting the craze

Invest in at least two or three crazes (more if your funds allow) and gradually build up your resources. Keep the craze in one part of the playground. It helps to contain the equipment, making it easier to collect. Have only one type of equipment each week. At the end of the week put it away and bring out what is needed for the next craze. This will enable you to keep the children's interest and rotate the equipment over a number of weeks.

> *We focused on skipping for a week and organised a skip-a-thon to raise money for more skipping ropes and as part of the national healthy heart campaign. It was a very effective way of raising the playtime profile, fundraising, sharing lots of skipping games and involving the whole school community in having fun and getting fit. Lots of teachers, supervisors and parents took part. I remember one boy watching his teacher and saying, 'Wow, Miss can skip!'*
>
> Head teacher

Playground Friends can help children use the equipment. It really helps if supervisors take part in the games too; for example, turning the rope in skipping encourages children to join in. Some children may need help to develop the skills necessary to use the equipment correctly and become able to play games sensibly; otherwise they run the risk of not being able to play with it at all.

Traditional playground games zone

To include the teaching of traditional playground games in the school's playtime policy it is vital to have the commitment and appropriate level of staff.

Many schools are re-introducing traditional playground games (see chapter 9). A supervisor and the Playground Friends can choose a game and focus on teaching it to as many children as possible for one week. It makes a difference, and adds status to the game, if the adult gets involved. Then children are more likely to join in. The Playground Friends may find it difficult to motivate children to play the game, but as soon as an adult starts to play it becomes more interesting. Once the game is established, children will continue to play it with their own friends and add their own variations too.

Friendship Stop zone

This is an area in the playground to which lonely children can go, sit on a bench, and wait for a Playground Friend to come and talk to them and help them find someone to play with. Playtimes can be very lonely for some children. They wander around with nothing to do and with no friends. Some find it hard to ask if they can join in a game. Others may be lonely because their best friend isn't in school. Knowing that they can go and sit on a special bench that has been designated for lonely children helps them to feel less isolated. Some schools paint a bench in bright colours and install a wooden lollipop that says 'Friendship Stop'. The bench gives a positive message to parents and other visitors to the school about the caring ethos of the playground.

It is important that the Playground Friends speak to the children in a friendly and non-aggressive manner.

Quiet zone

This is an area that is used for quiet activities and relaxation. Some schools use a garden area as their quiet zone. You may have benches or seats already arranged in such an area, or you can put carpet tiles down each day. This area is specifically for such things as quiet chats, reading, board games and activity books. The equipment can be stored in a box. The children using the area and the Playground Friends ensure that it is returned to the box at the end of playtime.

Make-believe zone

Children love dressing up – it is popular with all children, regardless of their age. Items of clothing and accessories to be worn over the children's own clothes – for example, hats, dresses, gloves, shawls, bags, jackets and waistcoats – are provided in a box. Net curtains are also ideal. Advertise for items in your school newsletter or on the parents' notice board.

Music and dance zone

A zone in the playground for dancing and listening to music has proved incredibly successful, especially with the older year groups. Ask children to suggest songs and music for the collection; they are the best judges of what will be popular. Keep everything in a box that is returned to the store cupboard at the end of playtime. Some schools have a big tape/CD player used by supervisors who lead keep-fit sessions in the playground.

Children may like to try some busking during playtime. This is also a good opportunity for pupils to develop their performance skills.

> *We have a CD player that is used at playtimes. We were going to have it out occasionally, but it has proved so popular that we use it every day. It is used mainly by the girls and a few boys to learn new dance steps and routines.*
>
> Supervisor

Parachute zone

This is an area where parachute games take place. Parachute games are cooperative activities that provide an ideal opportunity for fun and enjoyment. It is best to spend some time with your supervisors initially, teaching them how to use the parachute to make ripples and mushrooms and to play some parachute games.

A few parachute games to get you started

When they play parachute games children may be over-enthusiastic, so you need to devise an effective way to gain their attention when you need to. One easy way is to ask them to repeat the word 'Stop' when you say it, then to stand still. With practice they will be able to do this quickly and calmly.

Shout 'Hello'

The children stand around the parachute, holding it at waist height. On the count of 3, they raise their arms to make the parachute mushroom and shout 'Hello' to the person opposite.

Greetings

The children stand around the parachute, holding it at waist height. Two children from opposite sides are chosen to perform a greeting underneath the parachute; for example, shake hands, give a high five, touch elbow to elbow. On the count of 3, the children raise their arms to make the parachute mushroom. The two chosen children run underneath the parachute to the centre, perform their greeting and then swap places.

Change places

The children stand around the parachute, holding it at waist height. The adult calls out a category; for example, anyone with black shoes, anyone wearing red. Try not to make the categories too broad; otherwise there will be nobody left to hold the parachute! On the count of 3, the children raise their arms to make the parachute mushroom. Any children in the specified category have to swap places underneath the parachute.

Underground tunnels

The children sit or crouch around the parachute, which is on the ground. A child is chosen to name someone on the other side of the circle. Both children then crawl under the parachute and tunnel in the direction of each other. The other children ripple and shake the parachute, keeping it low and trying to disorientate the tunnellers.

Construction and small equipment zone

This is an area that can be used for playing with construction toys and other small equipment, such as plastic or wooden bricks, marbles, chalk, paper and crayons.

> *We had a construction kit that we used for 'wacky races'. Children worked in teams to build vehicles and race them. On other days they would build smaller vehicles and work together in teams to complete them.*
>
> Supervisor

Chalk boards

Some schools have a large blackboard that the children can use. Others have individual ones. Chalk and cloths need to be provided. Children can be encouraged to take part in drawing competitions, the winners being allowed to chalk their designs on the playground.

Performance zone

Many schools build a small stage on which to perform plays. This may be a project in which your PTA could become involved by fundraising, or by helping the children to design and build a stage for your playground.

Free-play zone

In addition to providing a range of specific activity areas, it is important to keep a free-play area where children can invent and play their own games.

Painted games zones

You may have access to a paint marking machine or, if your school budget and fundraising allows, you could commission some professional paint markings. You could organise a competition to think up new designs with prizes for the children. Many of the games, as well as being great fun, can be used for delivering aspects of the curriculum. For example, counting and alphabet games can be played on suitable markings. It is really important to help the children to learn how to use the game markings. Children may make up their own games, but often the markings are forgotten and become a greatly under-used resource. Design your markings carefully so that they do not interfere with the other zones.

> *We organised a competition for children and staff to design playground games and we displayed the entries around the school. We chose the winning design, which was then painted on the playground.*
>
> *Head teacher*

Last, but not least, the football zone – or shall we ban it?

Football may influence the ethos of your school. It is especially important that when you start zoning you consider having a football zone as this can change the whole dynamics of your playground. It will enable you to establish rules and routines so football doesn't dominate the playground. With regard to football it is worth asking the following questions:

★   What are some children learning about our school values?

★   Does the football squad consist mostly of older, stronger and more dominant boys, and are the younger, weaker children or the girls excluded?

★   Does football dominate most of the playground, and are the other children and adults frequently hurt by the ball?

If a handful of boys are allowed to dominate football, the hidden message given to the children may be that when resources are limited (small playground space, no equipment) they are given to the strongest and largest males. This results in bad gender images and contravenes any equal opportunities policy. Some schools avoid tackling this problem because of worries that older boys, if deprived of their football, will engage in antisocial activities, such as forming gangs to bully other children. A sound football policy is an essential part of reflecting the caring values promoted in a whole-school policy for self-esteem and positive behaviour.

Developing a football policy

Step 1

First identify a clearly zoned area where football may take place (some schools have two areas, one for Key Stage 1 and one for the Key Stage 2).

Step 2

Decide what your aim or statement is; for example, all children should be able to play football regardless of ability, age or gender.

Step 3

Agree rules and sanctions and how to organise the football rota.

Whatever your school decides, it's really important that the children and the playground staff are part of the process. The children are much more likely to stick to the rules if they have had a say in devising them. This can be done in a number of ways. Here are two examples:

★   Invite all children who wish to play football to attend a meeting once a term with teachers and lunchtime supervisors to agree rules and sanctions.

★   Each class discusses any ideas for rules and sanctions during a Circle Time meeting. One or two representatives from each class attend a meeting with the head teacher and lunchtime supervisors to discuss and agree upon them.

Examples of rules

★   Enjoy the game and don't spoil it for others

★   Anyone wearing a special football badge can play

★   No swearing

★   No put-downs.

Agreeing who plays and when

This could include:

★   a daily class football rota

★   two year groups playing on each day

★   a football-free day once a week

★   the class or group that has been best behaved on the rota has an extra turn on Friday

★   a girls-only football day, as this group is often under-represented

★   everyone who wants can play

★   writing a contract and asking children who want to play football to sign it – keep a copy in each class and have one for the playground staff (see page 189).

If you have a football rota, make sure that it is clearly displayed near the football area so everyone can see it. The advantage of everyone playing who wants to play is that you don't have to make sure who is allowed to on a specific day; the disadvantage is that there may be too many players.

There are many football clubs that organise community sports programmes in schools. It may be possible to arrange a lunchtime football club for your school. Some clubs provide this service to schools free of charge; others charge a fee.

Developing a football zone

The head teacher of a primary school decided to ban football because she was fed up with the behaviour of many of the children who were playing. The behaviour was very aggressive. Many of the players were being physically and verbally abusive towards each other. She asked us to work with the children to see if we could resolve the situation.

We had a meeting with the Playground Friends (some of whom played football) and a supervisor to discuss the problem. We asked the children the following questions:

Why was football banned?

★ Because there were too many fights over football

★ Fights started because the winning team would chant loudly and boast to the losing team

★ Children would argue about fouls and didn't work together as a team.

What was the effect in the playground when football was banned?

★ Children were rude to staff on duty

★ There were more playground fights

★ Some children were bullying others because there was nothing else to do.

What can we do to have the ban lifted?

★ Ban the children who cause the trouble

★ Have clear rules for football.

The questions and answers were distributed to all classes, and children were asked to comment and suggest ideas to make it possible to lift the ban. Some teachers used Circle Time to discuss this, while others discussed it informally.

We collected the comments and ideas, which were discussed with the head teacher, and we wrote a set of rules that we showed to the group.

→

Our football rules were:

★ Enjoy the game and don't spoil it for others

★ Don't laugh or chant at the losing team

★ Don't shout nasty names

★ Don't kick or hurt others.

The following sanctions were employed.

If you break any rules the following will happen:

★ Your name will go into the football book

★ If your name is written in the football book three times in a week you will have a football ban for a week.

So if you want to play football in your school, remember to keep the rules!

A contract was written up and sent to all classes. The children who wanted to play football had to agree to the rules and sign their names.

This process took about three weeks from the ban being implemented to its being lifted. The school was fortunate to have a large playground in which all children could play every day. Most children were able to play by the rules. A minority lost their football time.

Since this system was introduced the book has been replaced with playground sanctions that the school now uses. They have very few football incidents.

In addition to this, links have been developed with Leyton Orient Football Club, who come in twice a week and run a lunchtime football club for the Key Stage 2 children. The children have benefited enormously and have learned how to work in teams and develop their football skills.

Bigger things

Zoning is a low-cost and productive way of introducing effective activities and systems to the playground. It will produce positive changes in behaviour with a relatively small budget. When you have established your zones, you may want to concentrate on developing the playground's physical layout. Some schools have:

★ added murals

★ planted shrubs and flowers

★ involved landscape gardeners in developing outside classrooms

★ built activity runs

★ developed nature areas

★ created mosaics.

Frequently asked questions

How can we zone the playground, as we have separate playgrounds for Key Stage 1 and Key Stage 2?

You could divide the space into two sets of zoned areas, or merge the playgrounds into one.

> *When the idea of merging was suggested, we thought the older children would overwhelm the younger children. But once the zoned areas were introduced it wasn't an issue as children were occupied, and some of the younger ones liked being with the older ones and vice versa.*
>
> Supervisor

What if there are too many zones to manage?

If you have too many zones you may have started off too enthusiastically. You will have lots of equipment that it may be difficult to collect at the end of playtime; children may be flitting from one area to another and not focusing on what they are doing. It is best to start with three zones, gradually introducing more.

What if the craze of the week is very popular; can't we keep it for longer?

It helps to keep interest in the long run if you change the craze on a weekly basis. But find out what works best for your school.

ZONING THE PLAYGROUND

Task	Have you:	Resources you may need	Person responsible/ monitored by	Estimated cost	Review date
Divide the playground into zoned activity areas	• introduced the idea of zoned activity areas to supervisors? • drawn a map of your playground? • asked supervisors to write what each area is used for at present? • discussed with the supervisors how the zones should be organised?	• map of your playground			
Mark out the zones	• decided what you will use to divide the zones?	• chalk • shrubs • benches • cones • trees • paint			
Develop a craze of the week zone	• collected equipment to start your craze with? • prepared a notice to tell people what the craze of the week is? • organised Playground Friends to teach the craze?	• notice saying 'The craze of the week is ...' • hula hoops • skipping ropes • french skipping elastics • bats and balls • bean bags			

→

Task	Have you:	Resources you may need	Person responsible/ monitored by	Estimated cost	Review date
Develop a traditional games zone	• photocopied games onto card and laminated them? • arranged for a supervisor and Playground Friends to teach at least one different game each week?	• laminated game cards • place to keep them in			
Establish a Friendship Stop	• decided where the Friendship Stop will go?	• bench • Friendship Stop			
Develop a quiet zone	• identified a quiet space for the children? • provided enough seating? • asked parents to contribute magazines and old books?	• chalk • paper • crayons • magazines and books • seating • carpet squares			
Get a dressing-up box	• collected a box of dressing-up clothes and accessories? • used your school newsletter to ask parents for items? • put a notice on the parents' notice board?	• dressing-up clothes • handbags • purses • scarves			

→

ZONING THE PLAYGROUND

Task	Have you:	Resources you may need	Person responsible/ monitored by	Estimated cost	Review date
Develop a music and dance area	• got a tape/CD player? • asked children to suggest some songs for your selection? • a selection of tapes? • a secure place to keep everything?	• CD player • tape recorder • tapes • CDs			
Get some blackboards	• got blackboards?	• blackboards • chalk • cloths			
Develop a performance stage	• thought of having a small stage area?	• materials such as wood, nails, glue • volunteers to build stage			
Develop a football policy	• identified what the football problems are? • decided how you will determine the football rules and sanctions? • organised a meeting with those people involved? • written up the agreed football rules and sanctions? • displayed the football rules and rota in the football zone? • written a contract and asked children who want to play football to agree and sign it? • put a copy of the contract in each class and a copy in a folder for the playground staff?	• rules • contract • folder			

→

Task	Have you:	Resources you may need	Person responsible/ monitored by	Estimated cost	Review date
Paint some markings for games on the playground	• encouraged participation by involving the children and staff in a competition to design playground markings?	• game marking machine • professional paint markers • paint			
Establish a storage space and system for looking after the equipment	• a secure place for storing the equipment and resources? • Playground Friends responsible for putting the equipment away?	• cupboard with key • shed • lockable room			
Develop a system for replenishing equipment	• a system for regularly topping up your equipment?	• budget for new equipment			

7 | *Lunchtime – some practical suggestions*

It is no mean achievement that every day, in the space of an hour and a half, between 200 and 500 children may pass through a school dining hall and eat a cooked dinner or a packed lunch there. Your system has to be incredibly efficient to achieve a calm lunchtime. We shall outline some ways for you to explore and improve lunchtimes in your school in this chapter.

Lunchtime rules

First of all, your lunchtime rules need to be discussed and agreed with supervisors and children. They should be displayed clearly next to your school or Golden Rules in the dining hall. Ask children to draw pictures to go with them to represent the different rules.

For example:

▶   We line up quietly

▶   We walk in the dining hall

▶   We finish what we are eating before we speak

▶   We remember to say 'please' and 'thank you'

▶   We put our rubbish in the bin

▶   We put our hands up to ask to leave the hall.

Reviewing your systems

Regular meetings with lunchtime supervisors and catering staff, as well as observation of the lunchtime system, will help you identify and address key issues. The lunchtime audit on page 188 will help your discussions.

Supporting catering staff

Very often the catering staff are not seen as part of the school community, whereas supervisors who might work in classes are seen as part of the school. Catering staff are often neglected and they are very rarely, if ever, invited to assemblies or school social events. They are vital to the running of a good system; having the meals ready and serving them on time and with a smile is a crucial part of the lunchtime system. Even a 5-minute delay may have a domino effect and ruin the smooth running of lunchtime.

The chances are that your lunchtime supervisors will go on to playground duty when children have left the dining hall. A large number of children may not be adequately supervised in the playground sometimes because there are still children in the dining hall.

In many schools private catering companies prepare and serve the food, and it is vital that there is good communication between them and the lunchime supervisors to address any issues that arise.

How can we improve the relationship and communication with catering staff?

▶ Allow them to award Stars of the week to well-behaved children (see page 190)

▶ Invite them to special assemblies about lunchtimes

▶ Give them copies of the school newsletter

▶ Invite them to school celebrations

▶ Provide name badges for them, so when children say 'thank you' they can use the individual's name

▶ Give them access to incentives and sanctions

▶ Allow them to nominate one child each week who has consistently kept the lunchtime rules

▶ Ask for their ideas about improving lunchtimes.

CASE STUDY
One school's lunchtime problems

The school is gradually becoming a two-form entry school. This year they had two extra classes. Catering staff were asked to put out extra tables and chairs. They put out enough chairs for the children, but stopped short of putting out chairs for the supervisors. This caused a big upset.

> *How can we encourage the children to eat a bit more of their dinner and show them by example how to eat properly, if we are standing up eating and looking down at them all the time?*
>
> Supervisor

The cook was under pressure because of the increased amount of food she needed to prepare. She needed more staff in the kitchen. The school was awaiting additional funding from the local authority. Meanwhile, this was having an adverse effect on staff and on the system. The head teacher was able to organise a meeting with the cook to discuss her concerns. The situation has been resolved; there are now enough tables and chairs for the supervisors, and an extra member of staff for the kitchen has been promised.

Lining up

It is important to establish orderly and quiet entry into the dining hall. Younger and more timid children may find noise and jostling intimidating; consequently lunchtimes become a frightening experience for them. The wish to get their lunch and have a playtime may be very stressful for some children. Sometimes a small change can make a big difference. It may be wise to send children out to play and then call them in to eat, rather than have them queuing up for ages. When children line up to enter the dining hall a supervisor could gently remind them of the lunchtime rules.

Staffing issues

If a supervisor is absent from work, do you have a back-up system so that you can ask other members of staff to cover? It is important to recognise that the supervisors will have to work much harder to keep an orderly and calm lunchtime if they are one short. Support them by informing them if someone is absent and where possible offer help; that goes a long way in showing that you value them and the work they do. Don't just let them get on with it.

New reception class

During the first two weeks of a new reception class joining the school it is very important to introduce the children gradually to the dining hall rules and routines. Many of the children will have come straight from nursery or pre-school group to a larger, busier environment. To a 4-year-old it can be a daunting, noisy and intimidating experience to be in a hall with what seems like an enormous number of people.

Having a period of induction for children will:

▶ assist in making the transition from nursery and pre-school group as smooth and peaceful as possible

▶ give them an opportunity to get to know the supervisors and catering staff

▶ help them familiarise themselves with the rules and routines of the dining hall.

Investing time and additional support at this point will have a positive effect on your system. Part of the induction period could involve new children being 'adopted' by children from Year 6.

Staff in the dining hall

The presence of teaching and senior management staff, as well as supervisors, eating their lunch in the dining hall brings a sense of continuity to the school day for children. It also extends the positive social interaction between staff and children and helps to reinforce the high expectations of behaviour maintained elsewhere in the school.

Gaining quiet

The hands-up system is very effective. It works best when it is also practised in class and during assembly. The supervisor raises their hand and the children follow suit, at the same time becoming silent (younger children can place a finger on their lips). If occasionally the supervisor's hand is raised, not to gain quiet, but to give out a reward to a quiet child, the children are likely to have a positive approach to this system.

Another effective way of gaining quiet is to shake little bells and put a sandtimer on a ledge so the children can see how quickly they can achieve quiet.

Trays

To minimise time spent collecting lunch, some schools provide each child with an 'aeroplane tray' that contains both courses. Alternatively, the supervisors could wheel a trolley round to dispense the next course, avoiding the waste of time in lining up twice.

Music

Some lunchtime supervisors introduce at lunchtime calming music that the school plays in assembly. Decide what is best for your school; some halls have better acoustics than others.

Slow eaters

Some schools recognise that particular children are naturally slow eaters and provide a table they can move to before the second sitting comes in.

Family grouping

Some schools twin classes of older and younger children, so that each older child will look after a younger child whilst lining up, and if necessary help them cut up food and clear plates and cutlery.

In one school with 460 children the head teacher does the following in Key Stage 2. At the beginning of each year children are assigned to tables, and each table has a card on it showing their names. There is a mix of older and younger Key Stage 2 children on each table. The children stay on the table for a term or the whole year.

You can allow each child to enjoy a 'head of the family' role, signified by a special badge, on a rota basis.

Make learning about manners fun

Many families no longer sit down and have meals together in the home. A TV dinner doesn't encourage social interaction or good table manners. Drama is an excellent tool for learning about eating as a group, helping children to identify acceptable and unacceptable behaviour. Role play is especially important for those children who do not receive any informal training in table manners at home and who therefore might not perceive their behaviour as unacceptable. Children can show their role plays in assembly.

Use drama and role play to set up a restaurant or a café. You can have real cutlery and pretend food, or have real food as part of a food project with menus, tablecloths, waiters and waitresses.

Set up a café in your class, invite parents to have tea and biscuits and encourage children to show off their good manners.

Role-play the following scenarios and discuss behaviour that would be more acceptable.

▶ speaking with your mouth full

▶ not eating with a knife and fork

▶ shouting across the table

▶ saying unkind things about someone's food

▶ sharing food.

Safety – fire alarms

Have you practised the fire drill during lunchtime? The thought of evacuating the building during this time may sound horrific, but everyone should be clear about how to do it safely.

Using incentives to help children keep the rules and routines

Reinforcing the rules

To help reinforce your rules it is important to have clear incentives as well as sanctions in your dining hall. These should be part of your whole-school behaviour policy. In addition to the incentives and sanctions already covered in this book, here are three to use in the dining hall:

▶ lunchtime responsibilities or duties

▶ table of the week

▶ a whole-school visual display.

Lunchtime duties for the children

Lunchtime duties help to encourage responsible behaviour. Some children love doing jobs in the dining hall. These include wiping tables, filling the water jugs, sitting with children who need help cutting up their food, laying out the cutlery and scraping the plates. The last is a particularly popular job!

The Playground Friends can do these jobs but you may also ask children who look a bit lost or lonely to help. Children who can be very disruptive during lunchtimes find it calming to do jobs for an adult. This works particularly well if there is a positive relationship between the child and the supervisor, and it can help raise the child's self-esteem.

Table of the week

A special table is attractively set up with a tablecloth, jug of juice or sparkling water instead of tap water and a vase of flowers (artificial ones are fine). It is used on a weekly basis as a privilege for children who have kept the lunchtime rules.

Have a different focus each week; for example, good table manners or lining up well. Each week a number of children are invited to sit at the special table. When this idea was first introduced in one school it started off well, then deteriorated. We found out that it wasn't seen as a big incentive because children were separated from their friends. So the invitations were extended to include a friend, which made it a special experience. You will need a special table of the week for each sitting.

Visual display area to celebrate whole-school achievement

Many schools have whole-school assemblies each week at which they celebrate successes, with a focus on children's personal, social and academic achievements. This can be extended to include recognising children who are positive role models at lunchtimes and playtimes. A number of children are nominated each week by the supervisors for good dining-hall behaviour, or for keeping the rule of the week. These names are shown in an eye-catching display in the dining hall, with a different theme for each half-term or term, such as:

▶ bare tree, which has leaves added to it showing the names of children who have kept a rule; each leaf also has on it the rule/behaviour achieved.

▶ a lemon or apple tree with children's names written on lemons or apples (see pages 191 and 192)

▶ painted flower stems with children's names written on cut-out flowers

▶ an ocean picture with children's names written on cut-out fish

▶ a sky with children's names written on cut-out stars and planets.

Celebrating can be extended to include all staff, in particular the supervisors and catering staff. For instance, you could nominate the cook as Star of the week for her delicious puddings.

Names are called out in assembly and added to the display. Over the weeks this will grow and eventually be complete. If the hall is used for assemblies, this will enable parents, governors and other visitors to your school to see this celebration of the successes of all members of the school community.

Sanctions

Please refer to chapter 2.

CASE STUDY
How one primary school tackled a queuing problem

The upper Key Stage 2 classes would start lining up in the playground at 12.30 ready to go in for their lunch, which was at 12.45. Many of the children refused to go and play for 15 minutes because they wanted to be first in the line. The result was that for 15 minutes children would be pushing and shoving each other until it was time for them to go into the dining hall.

→

CASE STUDY

This caused major problems for the supervisors. They expressed a real concern about this and felt that they were spending their time policing the lines. The children had no respect for them, were rude and ignored their instructions. We suggested that we should try to find a solution. Morale was at a very low ebb. One supervisor said, 'They won't change. It's their attitude and there is nothing you can do.'

A few days earlier we had observed another school using a system for calling children in for lunch. We discussed this with the supervisors and, although they were not over-enthusiastic, they agreed to give it a try. To quote a supervisor, 'We have nothing to lose, and it might just work.'

The system was very simple.

First step: We typed up the name of each class in big letters on coloured card and laminated them. A supervisor kindly volunteered to do the typing on her computer at home.

Second step: We had an assembly where a supervisor and the head teacher explained that we were not happy with lunchtime lining up and we were going to try out a new idea. We had a test run, showing the children the cards in assembly and asking them to put their hands up when they saw the card for their class.

Third step: We put the plan into action. In the first week, a supervisor went down to the playground, rang the bell and held up one of the cards. Only those children in that class lined up. They went straight into the dining hall.

Fourth step: We adapted this to meet our needs. This meant that in the second week the supervisor didn't even have to go down to get the children. She put her head out of the dining-hall window, rang the bell and held up a card.

> *It's so much better; if there is any silliness or moaning in the line, I say, 'I can put your card at the bottom of the pile and send you all away' and that's all it takes for them to stop.*
>
> *Supervisor*

This system has been going for nearly a year and it is still as effective as when we started. Addressing the issue has had a big impact, creating calmer lunchtimes in which children and supervisors are much more relaxed. Listening to supervisors'

→

concerns, and addressing them in a proactive way, gave them a voice and an opportunity to be involved as key players in the change and improvement process. This in turn helped to raise their status and authority with the children.

The price of laminating ten cards was about £3. The cost of not addressing this issue would have been severe wear and tear on adults' nerves.

LUNCHTIME – SOME PRACTICAL SUGGESTIONS

Task	Have you:	Resources you may need	Person responsible/ monitored by	Estimated cost	Review date
Establish lunchtime rules	● agreed and displayed the lunchtime rules?	● paper ● laminated card			
Review your systems	● organised regular meetings with supervisors? ● completed the lunchtime audit?	● lunchtime audit ● budget for meetings			
Include catering staff	● organised meetings with the cook and/or all catering staff? ● discussed with catering staff any incentives and sanctions they would like to use? ● invited them to assemblies and school celebrations? ● celebrated their achievements? ● asked if they would like to wear name badges?	● suitable incentives and sanctions ● name badges			
Improve lining-up system	● an organised queuing system?	● laminated cards			

→

Task	Have you:	Resources you may need	Person responsible/ monitored by	Estimated cost	Review date
Address staffing issues	• a procedure for informing staff about absent colleagues? • a back-up support system to cover for absent staff?	• notice board			
Induction for new reception class	• established an induction period for the reception class? • invited Year 6 children to adopt the reception children?	• class lists			
Have an orderly lunchtime	• considered inviting staff to eat their lunch in the dining hall? • considered using aeroplane trays to stop the need to queue twice? • thought of using calming background music? • set up a table slow eaters can move to if they need more time to finish? • thought of family groupings at tables? • instituted a system for gaining quiet?	• aeroplane trays • tape/CD player • music • extra table • names of family groups			
Use drama and role play	• role-played scenarios in class? • used food as a cross-curriculum project to make a restaurant or café?	• menu • cutlery • tablecloth • pretend food • real food			

→

LUNCHTIME – SOME PRACTICAL SUGGESTIONS

Task	Have you:	Resources you may need	Person responsible/ monitored by	Estimated cost	Review date
Practise safety procedures	• clarified procedures for evacuating the building during lunchtime in the event of a fire alarm?	• clear instructions displayed around the school • copies of in- structions for each supervisor			
Introduce lunchtime incentives	• agreed the incentives to be used at lunchtimes with supervisors? • a list of lunchtime duties for some children? • considered using a visual display on a different theme each term to recognise children who keep the lunchtime rules? • considered a special table of the week? • written a list of duties of the Playground Friends in the dining hall?	• display for recog- nising children who keep lunchtime rules • tablecloth • jug • flowers • list of duties			
Introduce sanctions	• agreed the sanctions to be used in the dining hall?	• 'I am disappointed' notelets • 'I am disappointed' monitoring form			

8 | *Wet playtimes*

Wet playtimes can be noisy, chaotic misery for teachers, supervisors and children if activities to occupy the children are inadequate. An effective wet playtime is one for which there is a clear, easy-to-manage system in place, in which the children are engaged in an activity or playing well together, and there is little disruptive behaviour.

When we first began working with supervisors to improve wet playtimes in their schools, there was little or no optimism. Time is not spent on improving wet playtimes, partly because it seems to be low down on the list of priorities for busy schools. There may be a gloomy acceptance that it will be dreadful, because the children have to stay inside.

Bad wet playtimes can have a negative impact on the rest of the school day for the children — as well as the support and teaching staff, who have to manage wet playtime and its aftermath.

Wet playtime observations

It is always a good idea to observe a wet playtime before a meeting with supervisors to look at the general organisation and the activities and resources available to the children. Better still, take part in supervising a wet playtime and get a feel for what it's like. At the end of lunchtime you might feel like wearing a badge saying, 'I did wet playtime and survived.' Never underestimate the stress and pressure supervisors are under during these times.

Meet with your supervisors

Use the meeting to acknowledge the difficult job the supervisors have at wet playtime, as well as to focus on the key issues.

Decide on an indoor zoning system (see page 110) and make a list of all the resources you have that will help to address some of the concerns and issues.

Typical issues are:

- not enough games
- not enough space
- minority of children running around and disrupting other children's play
- too noisy
- not enough staff.

Maintain your resources and activities

Initially you may need to buy equipment for your wet playtimes. Some of it is likely to be used for outside activities as well. Make sure that you monitor and replenish stock on a regular basis and occasionally add new things. If you allow your stock to become depleted your school may not be able to invest the amount needed to bring it back to an effective level. It is especially important that an adult oversees the equipment to make sure it is used appropriately and to keep track of it.

Mornings and afternoons

Many children stay in their class with their teacher during wet playtimes. Each class should have a wet playtime box or area in their class containing a selection of the following:

- magazines and comics
- board games
- old greetings cards
- paper
- coloured pencils
- activity books.

In addition to this, many classes have a wet playtime book for each child to write or draw in which is kept in the child's drawer or in a box, and only used at that time. Some teachers have a written list of other resources and equipment the children are able to use. This gives the children and supervisor clear guidelines about what they can use, and prevents any arguments or misunderstandings.

Getting organised

Some schools allow children to stay in their class during wet lunchtimes. In this case the same routine as for wet mornings and afternoons will apply. Other schools use different parts of the school building at lunchtimes, such as a hall or video/television room, as well as some classrooms. This often depends on staffing levels during this period.

> *In our school the children stay in their classes until they have their lunch and return to their classes afterwards. Each class has a wet playtime box or area where wet playtime resources are kept. The supervisors monitor the classes and the corridor. This system works when the wet playtime box has things in it! Torn comics and pens that don't work are not very exciting for the children and will not be appreciated. I've noticed that the classes that have a good wet playtime box don't get their classrooms trashed.*
>
> Supervisor

Using a hall during wet playtime

Zoning a hall

The zoning system in a hall works on the same principle as in the playground, creating clear boundaries for a range of different activities. It is very important that you are organised and that the activities are out and ready before the children arrive in the hall.

> *Last week we were a bit late coming into the hall and the children were just behind us. It was chaotic because we weren't organised. The children came into an empty space. If there are activities ready for them it is much easier to engage them.*
> *So we try to get here a few minutes before the children and it usually works really well.*
>
> Supervisor

Storage

It is ideal to have a lockable cupboard in the hall where wet playtime resources can be kept, preferably with shelves and boxes labelled with the different activities and zone numbers. This makes it easy to see at a glance which boxes to take out. Write up a list of the zones and pin it up on the inside of the cupboard doors.

Create quieter areas by laying out a few PE mats on one side of the hall with quiet games and activities. These will encourage children to sit down when they enter the hall.

Below are examples of activities, divided into five zones. We suggest you have three zones only for each session and choose one activity from each. Too many zones in a relatively small space may well prove chaotic.

Inside zone 1

Craze of the day zone
Many of your craze of the week games can be played inside:

- french skipping
- bats and balls
- big hand tennis (very popular)
- hoop-la
- stilts
- parachute games.

Inside zone 2

Quiet game zone

- packs of cards
- dominoes
- chess sets
- draughts sets
- ludo
- Connect Four
- jacks.

Inside zone 3

Quiet activity zone

- old greetings cards
- magazines for collage
- box of quizzes and puzzle cards
- photocopied word searches
- colouring pencils and paper
- wet playtime story books.

Inside zone 4

Make-believe zone

- a bag of dressing-up clothes and accessories.

Inside zone 5

Traditional games zone

- indoor games printed on laminated card for use by the Playground Friends and supervisors.

Clubs/staff-led sessions

Some schools have a range of clubs or special staff-led sessions available during wet playtimes.

The clubs/sessions depend on having enough staff to take a group for a particular activity. These might include drama, art, ICT, music and dance. Teachers may volunteer to do a wet playtime club or session once a term. These can operate in a variety of ways. The most common is to draw up a list of clubs or sessions and who will take them, for wet playtimes. The list is displayed in the staffroom and also somewhere where the children can see it.

Teaching staff will be volunteering their help during this time and it would be unfair on them and the other children if a minority of children were disruptive and not able to follow the rules. It may be necessary for these children to be excluded.

Supervisors could take a year group out if the children have appropriate clothing for a run around.

Video

Some schools set up a video for classes on a rota system.

Playground Friends

Some schools have separate wet playtimes for Key Stage 1 and Key Stage 2. Your school may choose to have children from both key stages in the Playground Friends so there is always a group of children on duty. The Playground Friends can carry out the same duties as they would outside. They can read to younger children and help children with the quieter games and the craze of the week, as well as keeping the equipment within the appropriate zones and helping to put it away at the end of playtime.

Incentives and sanctions

The rewards and sanctions used at playtime apply. A minority of children find it very difficult to behave appropriately at playtime, and their behaviour may be very challenging to other children and to members of staff. Managing a wet playtime is difficult, and it is therefore crucial that your supervisors and the challenging child receive support during this time. In these circumstances, where possible, give the child special responsibilities for the session, such as doing errands and jobs for the head teacher, and reward them for doing so.

Key Stage 2 children often finish their lunchtime after the infants. You may be able to send a child into an infant class to help the younger children for 15–20 minutes.

End of playtime

Thankfully, there is an end to every wet playtime. Give yourself plenty of time to tidy up. A few minutes before the end of playtime blow the whistle or ring the bell. All children can start tidying up and putting the equipment away with the help of the Playground Friends.

Parents

Use your school newsletter, the parents' notice board or letters home to ask parents for contributions for wet playtimes, such as pieces of material, old greetings cards, buttons, sequins, and magazines for collage.

CASE STUDY
Inner city primary school

Our wet playtimes used to be horrible. The children were wild; they seemed to spend the whole time running up and down the hall and stairs. The toilets would be regularly flooded and the only activity was the video. Children would start fights and we couldn't wait until lunchtime was all over.

Supervisor

Time has been spent improving the system for wet playtime and the following system has been introduced:

- a TV room where one group of children watch a video.

A hall is used. In it there is a secure wet playtime cupboard with a selection of resources that are brought out when needed; for example:

- drawing
- collage
- board games
- craze of the day.

In addition to the above, they sometimes have music and dance, or access to the computers. This works on a class rota system that is written up in advance and is stuck on the inside of the cupboard door.

WET PLAYTIME ZONES

Choose three zones and take one activity from each.

ZONE 1 Craze of the day	ZONE 2 Quiet games zone	ZONE 3 Quiet activity zone	ZONE 4 Make-believe zone	ZONE 5 Traditional games zone
• skipping ropes • stilts • hoop-la • big hand tennis • soft balls • jacks	• packs of cards • dominoes • chess sets • draughts sets • ludo • board games	• old greetings cards • magazines for collage • box of quizzes and cards • photocopied word searches • colouring pencils and paper • wet playtime story books	• dressing-up clothes	• indoor games printed on card

→

Task	Have you:	Resources you may need	Person responsible/ monitored by	Estimated cost	Review date
Carry out a wet playtime observation/ audit	• looked at how wet playtime is managed? • identified what works well? • supervised a wet playtime session?				
Meet with supervisors	• listened to the concerns and issues about wet playtimes? • introduced the idea of zoning? • made a list of the resources you already have?	• a list of resources you already have			
Maintain your resources and activities	• someone to monitor your equipment? • a system for replenishing stock on a regular basis? • any playground activities that can be used for wet playtimes?	• someone responsible for monitoring and ordering new stock			
Plan wet playtimes	• a selection of zones to choose from? • a cupboard or storage space to keep equipment in? • a list of activities pinned to the door or somewhere else obvious? • a rota system for any clubs you may have?	• a list of activities • storage space • a rota for clubs			

→

WET PLAYTIME ZONES

Task	Have you:	Resources you may need	Person responsible/ monitored by	Estimated cost	Review date
Consider incentives and sanctions	● set up a range of incentives and sanctions supervisors can use? ● considered sending Key Stage 2 children into the infant classes for time out? ● given specific tasks to children who may find wet playtimes difficult to manage?	● mini-certificates ● stickers ● a range of incentives and sanctions			

9 | *Traditional playground games*

Why traditional games?

In the past, many traditional games were taught to younger children by older children, in the playground and, outside school, on the streets and in the park. One of the concerns at the present time is that our children live in a society that is heavily influenced by computers, television and videos. We are becoming a nation of couch potatoes who have everything done for us. Our children are not encouraged to use their imagination and to be inventive, except in relation to computer-orientated activities.

Parents are afraid for their children's safety and are reluctant to allow them to go outside and play with their friends in the park and streets after school. By bringing back some of the traditional games to your playground you can encourage children to:

★ interact socially with other children, not just their class or best friends

★ cooperate

★ take turns

★ develop speaking and listening skills

★ have fun

★ negotiate

★ learn the importance of rules

★ enjoy physical activity.

How to use the games

These games have been written in a style suitable for children to read and use with minimal help from adults. They are equally useful as a resource for staff, who can use them during PE or as part of their Circle Time games.

Curriculum links

If time is spent on playground games during PE or in other curriculum areas, the benefits can be seen in the playground, where children will be motivated to play them on their own.

Teachers have used the games in a variety of ways. In one school some games are played as a warm-up at the start of PE lessons. Another school focuses on one game per week. It is written out and displayed in the playground so that children can practise it at playtime. When a teacher has a 'tell a good tale' session after playtime, children have an opportunity to talk about what they have played.

It can be interesting to find out the significance of different games and what their origins are. The children could do a history project on them and present it in assembly.

Playground Friends

The Playground Friends can work with supervisors to teach children how to play the games. Once children learn to play them, they will invent and develop their own up-to-date versions.

And finally, about the games ...

When we were writing up 'What's the time, Mr Wolf?' we read a version of it and thought it didn't sound right. We asked some children what version they knew and, interestingly enough, they had learnt the version that we had learnt in school. There are many versions of some games. This doesn't matter. Children will develop and change them to suit their circumstances.

We were recently working with a teacher in class. We were teaching the children a ring dance called 'In and out the dusty bluebells'. It includes the line 'Who shall be my partner?' Two children who had learnt this at an out-of-school club corrected us by saying that the words were actually 'Who should be my master?' Our instinct was to teach them a version more in line with equal opportunities, but they preferred their own.

On another occasion, we were teaching some children how to play the game 'Oranges and Lemons'. When we came to the line '"I owe you five farthings", say the bells of St Martin's', a little girl sang it as '"I owe you five thousand", said the bells of St Martin's.' What a sign of inflation – and an opportunity to explain old currency!

List of games

1 What's the time, Mr Wolf?

1. Choose someone to be Mr Wolf.

2. Everybody else stands on a line on the playground, which is home, facing Mr Wolf.

3. Mr Wolf stands at the other end of the playing area with their back to the other players.

4. The players chant:

   What's the time, Mr Wolf?

5. Mr Wolf doesn't look, but says a time; for example:

   Eight o'clock.

6. The other players take eight steps forward, stop and chant:

   What's the time, Mr Wolf?

7. Mr Wolf says another time; for example:

   Three o'clock.

8. The others take three more steps, stop and chant:

   What's the time, Mr Wolf?

9. This continues until Mr Wolf turns and says:

   Dinner time.

10. He then chases everyone back home, trying to catch one of them.

11. A child who is caught becomes Mr Wolf and the game starts again.

12. If Mr Wolf does not catch anyone, they have to be Mr Wolf again.

13. If a player reaches Mr Wolf before dinner time, they tap Mr Wolf on the shoulder and run for home. Mr Wolf tries to catch a player in the same way as before.

2 Queeny, Queeny, who's got the ball?

1. Everybody stands together.

2. Someone is chosen to be a queen.

3. The Queen stands in front of the other players with their back to them.

4. The Queen throws a small soft ball over their shoulder.

5. One child catches it and everybody puts their hands behind their backs.

6. They then chant:

   Queeny, Queeny, who's got the ball?
   Are they short or are they tall?
   Queeny, Queeny, who's got the ball?

7. Queeny turns around, chooses someone and says:
   Have you got the ball?

8. If Queeny guesses incorrectly, that person becomes the Queen.

9. If Queeny gets it right, they throw the ball again.

10. The same person can be Queeny for a maximum of three games.

3 Who stole the cookies from the cookie jar?

1.   Everybody stands or sits in a circle.

2.   They all clap their hands and chant:

     Who stole the cookies from the cookie jar?

3.   A chosen player calls out another player's name; for example:

     Mary.

4.   Everybody claps their hands and chants:

     Mary stole the cookies from the cookie jar.

5.   Then Mary claps her hands and says:

     Who, me?

6.   The other players clap their hands and say:

     Yes, you.

7.   Mary claps her hands and says:

     Couldn't be.

8.   Everybody claps their hands and says:

     Then who?

9.   Mary claps her hands and calls out another name; for example:

     Ben.

10. Everyone claps their hands and says:

     Ben stole the cookies from the cookie jar.

11. The game continues as before.

4 **Follow the leader**

1. Everyone stands in a circle.

2. A detective is chosen.

3. The detective stands outside the circle with their back to everybody.

4. A leader is chosen, silently.

5. The detective moves to the centre of the circle.

6. The leader performs different actions that everyone else must copy.

7. The detective tries to guess who the leader is. They may make three guesses.

8. Whatever the result, a new leader and detective are chosen for the next round.

5 Duck, duck, goose

1. Everybody stands or sits in a circle.

2. A chosen player walks around the outside of the circle and touches each person in turn on the shoulder.

3. As they walk round, that person names each child they touch as follows:
   Duck, duck, duck.

4. At some point they say:
   Goose.

5. The goose then chases the namer round the circle.

6. They race to be the first back to the empty space.

7. The person who loses starts the next round.

6 Sheep, sheep, come home

1. One child is chosen to be a fox and another is chosen to be a farmer. The rest of the group are sheep.

2. All the sheep stand at one end of the game area. The farmer stands at the other end.

3. The fox stands in the middle.

4. The farmer says:
   Sheep, sheep, come home.

5. The sheep say:
   We're frightened of the fox.

6. The farmer says:
   The fox has gone to Devonshire and won't be back for seven year.

7. The sheep run to the farmer and the fox tries to catch one.

8. Any child who is caught either helps the fox as a catcher, or swaps places with the fox.

9. If they join the fox, the game ends when all the sheep have been caught.

7 Cat and mouse

1. One person is chosen to be the cat and another to be the mouse.

2. Everybody else stands in a circle and holds hands.

3. The cat stands outside the circle. The mouse is inside.

4. The cat has to try to catch the mouse by getting into the circle.

5. Those in the circle try to keep the cat away from the mouse by blocking any attempts to get near the mouse.

6. They can help the mouse by raising their arms to let them in and out of the circle.

7. This game can be played with two cats.

8 Oranges and lemons

1. Two children join hands and form an arch. Everybody sings the song:

   'Oranges and lemons'
   Say the bells of St Clement's.
   'I owe you five farthings'
   Say the bells of St Martin's.
   'When will you pay me?'
   Say the bells of Old Bailey.
   'When I grow rich'
   Say the bells of Shoreditch.
   'When will that be?'
   Say the bells of Stepney.
   'I do not know'
   Says the great bell of Bow.
   Here comes the candle to light you to bed.
   Here comes the chopper to chop off your head.
   Chip chop, chip chop, the last man's dead!

2. While this is being sung, the other children pass under the arch in a line. At the end of the rhyme the children forming the arch drop their arms and capture a child. That child goes behind one of the children in the arch and puts their hands on that child's shoulders or waist. The game continues until the last child is caught. This child then chooses a partner and they become the new arch for the next game.

   Here is an alternative ending to the traditional version above:

   Here comes the candle to light you to bed.
   Here comes a dream to fill your tired head.
   Sleep tight, sleep tight, the last word's said.

9 I sent a letter

1. Everybody holds hands and forms a circle.

2. One child is chosen to walk around the outside of the circle.

3. Everyone chants:
   I sent a letter to my friend and on the way I dropped it.
   Someone must have picked it up and put it in their pocket.

4. The child taps children in turn on the shoulder and says:
   It wasn't you.

5. Then they tap someone on the shoulder and say:
   It was you.

6. That person chases the caller around the circle and back to the empty space.

7. The child who gets there second starts the next game.

10 Creeping up on Grandma or Grandpa

1. Everybody stands at one end of the playing area.

2. Someone is chosen to be Grandma or Grandpa.

3. They go to the other end of the playing area and stand with their back to the other players.

4. The children take it in turns to try to creep up on Grandma/pa and touch their shoulder.

5. If Grandma/pa hears someone, they call out, 'I hear you' and that child has to go back to the others.

6. If a player manages to touch Grandma/pa, the game starts again with a new Grandma/pa.

11 Chinese whispers

1. Everybody stands in a circle.

2. One child begins by whispering a sentence to the person on their left.

3. That person whispers it to the person on their left.

4. This continues until it reaches the person on the right of the first child.

5. They say the sentence out loud and this is compared with the original message.

12 Spider's web

1. Everybody stands on one side of the playing area.

2. One person is chosen to be the spider.

3. The spider stands in the middle of the playing area.

4. The other players are numbered 1 or 2. They are the flies.

5. When the spider says 'One', all those children try to cross the playing area.

6. If the spider touches any of the flies, they are trapped in the spider's web and must stand still.

7. The children numbered 2 then must help release the trapped flies by touching them on the shoulder.

8. If the spider touches them they become trapped too.

9. The game ends when all the flies have been trapped or after an agreed time.

10. The last person to be trapped becomes the new spider.

11. This time the children numbered 2 go first.

13 **Peep behind the curtain**

1. Everybody stands at one end of the playing area.

2. One child is chosen to stand in front with their back to the others.

3. The rest of the players try to creep up behind the child in front and touch them on the shoulder.

4. The child in front can look round at any time, at which point the other children must freeze.

5. If they see anybody moving the person seen has to go back to the start.

6. The child who is the first to touch the child in front on the shoulder is the winner. They become the child in front and the game starts again.

7. If a child spots everybody creeping up on them they can have a second go. After this a new child is chosen to take their place.

14 The farmer's in his den

1. Everybody stands in a circle. One child is chosen as the farmer and stands in the middle.

2. The other children hold hands and walk round the circle, chanting:

   The farmer's in his den, the farmer's in his den, ee-i ee-i, the farmer's in his den.
   The farmer wants a wife, the farmer wants a wife, ee-i ee-i, the farmer wants a wife.

3. The farmer chooses a wife, who joins him in the middle.

4. Everybody else holds hands, walks round and chants:

   The wife wants a child, the wife wants a child, ee-i ee-i, the wife wants a child.

5. The wife chooses a child, who goes into the middle.

6. Everybody else walks round the circle and chants:

   The child wants a nurse, the child wants a nurse, ee-i ee-i, the child wants a nurse.

7. The child chooses a nurse, who goes into the middle.

8. Everybody else holds hands and chants:

   The nurse wants a dog, the nurse wants a dog, ee-i ee-i, the nurse wants a dog.

9. The nurse chooses a dog that goes into the middle.

10. Everybody else holds hands and chants:

    The dog wants a bone, the dog wants a bone, ee-i ee-i, the dog wants a bone.

11. The dog chooses a bone that goes into the middle.

12. Everyone gently pats the dog and chants:

    We all pat the dog, we all pat the dog, ee-i ee-i, we all pat the dog.

13. The bone becomes the farmer and the game begins again.

15 **Slips** (from Jamaica)

1. You need at least five children in each team.

2. The teams stand opposite each other.

3. There is a line dividing them – use playground markings or a skipping rope.

4. One team has a sponge ball.

5. Players in each team take it in turn to throw the ball and try to hit someone from the other team. The children have to try to get out of the ball's way.

6. If a player is hit they are out.

7. The game continues until every person in one team is out.

16 **In and out the dusty bluebells**

This is a ring dance for six or more children.

1. Everybody stands in a circle and holds hands. They raise their arms to make arches.

2. One child is chosen as a dancer.

3. The dancer goes in and out of the arches, while the other children sing:

   In and out the dusty bluebells
   In and out the dusty bluebells
   In and out the dusty bluebells
   Who shall be my partner?

4. When they sing 'Who shall be my partner?', the dancer taps whoever is closest on the shoulder and everyone sings:

   Tippity, tappity on your shoulder
   Tippity, tappity on your shoulder
   Tippity, tappity on your shoulder
   You shall be my partner.

5. This child becomes the new leader and the first child puts their hands on the leader's waist or shoulders and starts the song again.

6. Continue the dance until only two children are left, making an arch.

17 Teddy bear skipping game

1. Two chilDen turn a long skipping rope.

2. While one child skips in the middle, the other children line up and chant:

   Teddy Bear, teddy bear, touch the ground.

   Teddy Bear, teddy bear, turn around.

   Teddy Bear, teddy bear, show your shoe.

   Teddy Bear, teddy bear, that will do!

   Teddy Bear, teddy bear, run upstairs.

   Teddy Bear, teddy bear, say your prayers.

   Teddy Bear, teddy bear, blow out the light.

   Teddy Bear, teddy bear, say goodnight.

3. The child skipping must do an action for each line of the rhyme.

4. If the child successfully completes all the actions, they have a go at turning the rope.

5. If they don't complete the rhyme they join the end of the line waiting to skip.

18 Keeper, keeper, may we cross your golden river in your golden boat?

1. Everybody stands on a line at one end of the playing area.

2. A child is chosen to be the keeper, and stands in the middle of the playing area.

3. An imaginary golden river with a golden boat floating on it separates the players from the other side of the playing area.

4. The players chant:

    Keeper, keeper, may we cross your golden river in your golden boat?

5. The keeper chooses something some of the players have in common, and replies; for example, 'Only if you are wearing … a watch/the colour blue/trainers.'

6. Any players who fit the category cross to the other side.

7. The remaining players then try to get to the other side without being caught by the keeper.

8. Any player caught joins the keeper. The game continues until all the players have been caught.

19 **Sticky toffee**

1. A child is chosen to be the chaser.

2. The other players touch one of the chaser's fingers, remaining in contact with the chaser.

3. The chaser says a list of items that they bought from a shop. Each of these must begin with the word 'sticky'; for example:

    I went to a shop and bought some sticky sweets, some sticky orange juice, a sticky lolly, some sticky toffee.

4. When the players hear the words 'sticky toffee', they run away and the chaser tries to catch them.

5. A child who is caught has to stand still with their arms or legs apart.

    They can move when someone releases them from the sticky toffee by going through their legs or under an arm.

6. The game ends when everybody is stuck, or after an agreed time.

20 **Bingo**

1. Everybody stands in a circle.

2. One child is chosen to stand in the middle.

3. Everybody chants:

    There was a farmer, who had a dog
    and Bingo was his name-o.
    B-I-N-G-O.

4. For each letter chanted the child in the middle points to a different child round the circle. The child pointed to when the group chants the last letter joins the child in the middle. The game continues until one child is left, who starts the next game.

5. If there are not many children playing this game, the child pointed to at the end of the chant may swap places with the one in the middle.

TRADITIONAL PLAYGROUND GAMES

Task	Have you:	Resources you may need	Person responsible/ monitored by	Estimated cost	Review date
Introduce games into the curriculum	• given a set of games to each class? • discussed with staff the games being included as part of your PE curriculum? • included games in other parts of the curriculum, such as History or PSHE?	• copies of the games			
Use the Playground Friends to teach the games	• arranged for a supervisor and members of the Playground Friends to teach at least one game a week?	• copies of the games • place to keep the list of games you have			
Make the games accessible to the children in the playground	• made sure you have a set of games that are easily accessible to the children? • set up a system for returning them after they have finished playing them?	• copies of the games • place to keep the copies			

10 | *Working in partnership with parents and the wider community*

Involving parents and other members of the local community in your school can help build a good rapport with staff and develop positive links between home, school and the wider community.

Simply getting people together can have a profound effect on their own well-being and self-esteem.

Some of the parents in one school worked with a local artist to paint a mural that the children had designed on a playground shed:

> *I've really enjoyed it, and it's good for the children to see parents taking part.*
>
> *Parent*

Involving the children's parents

It is much easier to involve parents in small projects initially. To encourage parents to take part you can give children a list of jobs you need assistance with to take home, asking parents to tick one they can help with. If they do not have to make a long-term commitment to the school they are more likely to volunteer their help. Very often these parents end up working in a school indefinitely and are worth their weight in gold.

Example of a parent help list:

Dear parents,

Can you spare three hours this term?

Can you spare one hour a week to help us?

We are running a range of projects this term. Each project will last about three weeks, and we are asking parents to help for about one hour each week. The days and times can be agreed with the group.

We need a group of parents who can assist us with any of the following:

▶ A mini-art project in the playground

▶ Planting flowers in our playground

▶ Covering books

▶ Sharing some games you used to play during one of our Golden Times

▶ Making a puppet theatre

▶ Making some dressing-up clothes.

You could also send a letter to parents headed 'Can you help improve our lunchtimes?', requesting old games or equipment they have that is suitable for wet playtimes. You can also approach local businesses to ask them to make a contribution.

Sometimes, children are effective in encouraging their parents to come in to school and support their class.

In a school we know, Year 1 children wrote out invitations to parents, inviting them for a session of Bingo and a cup of tea at the Friday afternoon Golden Time. The invitations had to be returned with a tick in a box to indicate whether parents could come. The children were really enthusiastic and over half of the parents came. The children and parents had a great time and some parents volunteered to help out in Golden Time and other areas too.

Sharing your playtime and lunchtime policy with parents

Some schools summarise their playtime and lunchtime policy in an easy-to-read leaflet, explaining rules, routines, rewards and sanctions, as well as giving the names of supervisors on duty. The leaflet can be given to all children and later to any new children who join the school. It can be reviewed and updated on a yearly basis and given out at the beginning of each school year. Copies should be available for parents to take from a rack, if you have one, and displayed on the parents' notice board. See pages 193–194 for a sample leaflet.

> *I think the leaflet is really good because it tells me what they do at playtimes and I now understand about the rewards and the Playground Friends.*
>
> *Parent*

Involve your governors

Ask children to write a letter inviting a governor to a playtime. Alternatively, they can fill in an invitation card (see page 195). Children can adopt a governor for playtime, show them around and answer any questions they may have. The children might invite them back to their class for a Circle Time on playtimes. Encourage your governors to ask supervisors about the improvements and changes that have taken place and how they have made a difference to the way children and staff interact and behave towards each other. These visits will give your governors an insight into the real issues and give them a chance to listen to the people who use the playground. Hopefully when they discuss this at governors' meetings they can share their experiences with each other. This may enthuse them even more and encourage them to become involved in other events, such as the skip-a-thon, assemblies, quiz nights and international food evenings.

Parent/teacher association, home–school association and friends of the school

The role of these groups varies greatly from school to school and may include the following.

Fundraising and organising different school events

One of your groups may be interested in fundraising, or planning and organising a specific part of your playground action plan. Involving the whole school community can be exciting but also very time consuming. Some schools are able to raise large amounts of money whilst for others this is much harder. But such events do help funds, even in a small way, and can build an excellent sense of community. Funds raised could help with the following areas:

▶   plants and shrubs for your quiet area

▶   playground games equipment

▶   benches and tables.

PTA

If your school has a PTA, share your ideas with them. They may be interested in raising money for a specific part of your action plan.

Governors at meetings may have ideas about and ability to raise money for your school. People are much more likely to be supportive of your playground improvements if you are very clear about where the money will be spent. Equally, having the action plan will help your school to focus specifically on what you are trying to achieve.

> *I work for a bus company which was able to donate some model buses for our raffle.*
>
> *Governor*

A sponsored skip

This event will promote the importance of keeping fit, raising money for skipping ropes. The British Heart Foundation have a yearly sponsored skip, from which a percentage of the money goes to their funds and the rest to the school, as well as skipping ropes, tapes of music and a book of skipping games.

Playground Friends

The Playground Friends could have a stall at a school fete to raise money for the playground.

Raffles

You could include a raffle to raise funds in any of your school events, such as concerts, plays and fetes.

Quiz nights

Bringing the school community together with teams made up of children, staff, parents and governors is a great way to raise funds and have a good time.

International food evenings

These offer a great opportunity to celebrate the diverse cultures in your school. People donate a dish and everyone pays a set amount for a plate of food.

Plan a project

A group may be able to take responsibility for organising a project to collect stories and games parents and grandparents used to play. Invite a small group of parents and grandparents to come into school over a period of time and set up a project to collect traditional playground games they used to play. These could be recorded in some way. A video could become a school resource, and could be shown as part of an induction programme for new parents and children. You could use a tape/CD player to record parents and grandparents explaining the games. The recordings could be typed up and made into a booklet to raise funds. Display aspects of the project around the school and during open days and other events.

School shop

Many schools regularly sell educational resources at affordable prices.

Playground equipment, such as skipping ropes, soft balls, french skipping, jacks and stilts, can be sold too. This will encourage children to develop good patterns of play at home. It is also an effective way of raising funds.

Invite parents to playtimes

Children could give out special invitations asking their parents to come to school during playtimes one week each year or term to celebrate your achievements. You may want to show off a new piece of equipment or show your Playground Friends in action.

Examples of themes:

▶	Our quiet area is now complete; come and sit in the shade and read a
book with us.
▶	Have a tour of the playground with the Playground Friends and ask
	questions about the scheme.
▶	Come and talk to the children and find out what they think of playtimes.

Initially the idea of parents at playtime may fill you with horror. However, when parents come to school and see a typical playtime they often gain a better understanding of the difficulties faced during this time – in a typical playground you could have between 200 and 400 children with a handful of staff. A visit will only increase parents' respect for the work that the supervisors do.

If a parent has a question when they come to visit, they should be able to speak to the head teacher or another senior member of staff. They may have queries regarding health and safety, budget implications or staff training needs. If your school is taking a whole-school approach towards improvement and change, it is essential that these issues are addressed. In order to have a significant impact on playtimes, lines of communication with parents need to be open.

School newsletter

A school newsletter is a fantastic way of informing parents and carers about the progress and plans you have. If your school doesn't have a regular newsletter, consider one just for playtimes and send it out once a term, focusing on one aspect of your playtime development. Make it interesting and informative. It offers an ideal opportunity to request items such as dressing-up clothes, games for wet playtimes and old magazines.

You could ask a class to produce a newsletter. They could charge for a copy, the money going towards a specific playtime resource.

Children can write a poem or story about one aspect of playtime. It could be about:

- ▶ a lonely child
- ▶ someone who is being bullied
- ▶ how to keep fit in the playground
- ▶ their favourite game.

Ask children to take on the role of journalist and interview parents, grandparents, supervisors, Playground Friends and each other about such subjects as 'What games our parents and grandparents played at school' and 'A day in the life of a lunchtime supervisor'.

Interview questions for parents and grandparents
In which country did you go to school?
What games do you remember playing at school?
Were you ever lonely?
What is your best playtime memory?
What is your worst playtime memory?

Interview questions for the Playground Friends
Why did you become a Playground Friend?
How long have you been doing this job?
What do you like about it?
How do you know if someone is lonely?
What is the best thing about your job?
What do you do if you think someone is being bullied?

Interview questions for supervisors
What do you enjoy about your job?
What do you find difficult?
If you could change one thing about your job, what would it be?
What's the funniest thing that has ever happened to you in the playground?

Interview questions for children
What is your favourite game?
What is the best thing about playtimes?
If you could change one thing about playtimes, what would it be?

Very often parents only hear the bad things that have been happening to their child at playtime; presenting these interviews in a newsletter is a good way of redressing the balance.

Parents' notice board

Pin a copy of your newsletter on the board, along with requests for dressing-up clothes, games and magazines. Provide a box in the school entrance hall where people can leave their contributions.

Celebrating parents

Once a term invite parents to an assembly on successes at playtime. Publicly acknowledge and celebrate parents' involvement by giving out certificates (see page 196). Inform them in advance that they will be receiving a certificate to enable them to prepare themselves to stand in front of the whole school and be applauded. If they can't make the assembly, their child can receive their certificate on their behalf.

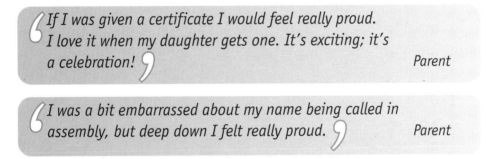

> *If I was given a certificate I would feel really proud. I love it when my daughter gets one. It's exciting; it's a celebration!*
>
> Parent

> *I was a bit embarrassed about my name being called in assembly, but deep down I felt really proud.*
>
> Parent

Social events to bring the school community together

► Sports day with activities for adults to take part in.

► Sponsored skip-a-thon in which everybody can take part.

► Focus on the school's grounds. Learning Through Landscapes, the national charity for schools, organise a school grounds week each year in conjunction with London Electricity. This encourages schools to focus on their grounds for a day or a week.

► Whole-school aerobics or keep-fit sessions to promote the importance of regular exercise.

► And, of course, your usual summer and Christmas concerts and events will be held.

Other ideas ...

There may be parents and other members of the community who have skills they would like to share with the children for a given period of time in such ways as the following:

►   Volunteers who work in old people's homes could come and talk to the children or show them how to play games.

►   Local churches may have a group of people who would like to come and help during playtimes.

►   Designing playground games and murals with the children and paint them on the walls and playground.

►   Local football clubs sometimes offer lunchtime football sessions.

INVOLVING PARENTS AND THE WIDER COMMUNITY

Task	Have you:	Resources you may need	Person responsible/ monitored by	Estimated cost	Review date
Involve parents	● made a checklist of jobs parents can volunteer to do? ● written a letter which is sent home, asking for help?	● a checklist of jobs ● a letter			
Develop a play-time and lunchtime policy	● considered developing a playtime and lunchtime policy in line with your behaviour and anti- bullying policy?	● meetings with staff and parents ● a draft policy			
Write a playtime and lunchtime leaflet for parents	● summarised the policy in leaflet form? ● distributed copies to all parents and governors? ● displayed it on the parents' notice board? ● kept spare copies in the office or on a rack?	● leaflets ● notice board ● spare leaflets			
Involve governors	● invited a governor to visit your school at playtime? ● included a governor in a working party on playtimes?	● invitations written by the children			

INVOLVING PARENTS AND THE WIDER COMMUNITY

Task	Have you:	Resources you may need	Person responsible/ monitored by	Estimated cost	Review date
Set up a fundraising group	● formed a group of parents interested in setting up a school shop? ● obtained a budget to get started if necessary? ● identified any support needed to do this? ● asked if anyone is interested in fundraising for a specific part of your playground plan? ● asked if any parents can set up a project to help collect playground games? ● gathered ideas for fundraising events?	● budget to get shop started ● copies of playground action plan ● letters to parents			
Invite parents to playtime	● given parents a special invitation to come in at playtime? ● set up a system for dealing with concerns from parents?	● invitations			
Writing a school newsletter	● considered a termly playground newsletter with contributions from the children? ● thought about the children producing the newsletter as a class project? ● asked children to interview the Playground Friends and support staff? ● asked children to interview their parents and grandparents about games they used to play?	● playground newsletter ● interview questions			

→

Task	Have you:	Resources you may need	Person responsible/ monitored by	Estimated cost	Review date
Put up a parents' notice board	● displayed information about playtimes? ● requested donations of dressing-up clothes, board games and magazines?				
Plan assemblies	● invited parents in to your termly/half-termly assembly on playtimes? ● given out certificates to parents at assemblies?	● parent certificates			

Organise social events	● organised regular social events in your school to highlight the playtimes through health initiatives and fundraising? Examples:
	  a skip-a-thon
	  aerobics
	  keep fit which can be done in the playground
	  summer and Christmas fairs
	  international food evenings
	  raffles
	  quiz
	  school concerts.				

External fundraising

In this chapter we present an example of a school's initiative to raise funds from external sources. On page 197 there is a form you can use to draw up your own master action plan.

CASE STUDY
One school's approach to applying for grants and fundraising for playtimes

We have a school roll of 318 children and at present we have a one-and-a-half form entry.

Over the last four years we have been implementing the Quality Circle Time model and have paid particular attention to improving playtimes in our school. When we first started, the playground was very bleak, with no resources for the children. The supervisors spent much of their playtimes managing difficult behaviour.

With the help of the head teacher we developed an action plan to help prioritise the changes and improvements we wanted to implement. This is an account of how we managed to raise money on the strength of the action plan. It includes letters used to support our application forms.

Step one

We looked at the Quality Circle Time model and decided which areas we wanted to focus on. We then used this information to write an action plan with clear aims that we wanted to achieve.

→

CASE STUDY

Step two

We found out where we could apply for funding. The main source was the national school grounds charity, Learning Through Landscapes. They were also able to tell us about other organisations that we could apply to.

Step three

Each time we applied for funding we included a copy of our playground newsletter and an action plan for the whole project. We highlighted the specific areas we were requesting the funding for. When writing the letters we were very specific about how we were going to spend the money in the context of the wider plan.

Applying for funding is time consuming, but having a clear structure for applying really helped us achieve many of our goals. We have received over £8000 in the past four years and 80% of our applications have been successful. The action plan really enabled us to focus on a particular aspect and apply accordingly.

St John's Primary School

Carling Road Cambridge CB6 7PQ

Mr A. Smith
125 City Road
Cambridge
CB7 6ZT

7 March 2001

Dear Mr Smith

RE: Grant Application for Improving the Educational Environment

Thank you for your letter inviting us to apply for a grant to help us to improve our educational environment. We would like to apply for a grant to help us develop the quiet area in our playground. Our school is a primary school with approximately 280 children on the school roll. It is in a large three-storey Victorian building and has a sizeable playground on three sides.

Since September 1999 we have developed a playground action plan with clear aims and objectives (enclosed). Our school has been implementing the Quality Circle Time model of behaviour. This model takes a whole-school approach to self-esteem building and behavioural management that extends from the school building to the playground. It is clear from our experience that negative experiences on the playground are transferred to the classroom. This can have a very disruptive effect that can affect the whole teaching and learning environment. The grant we are applying for will enable us to develop a quiet zone in our playground.

At present, the quiet zone is in a walled-off area of the playground that has raised flowerbeds and two benches built into the walls. It is a very unfriendly space with red brick walls, sharp corners and an array of rather sad-looking plants. It has two entrances, which encourages pupils to run through it rather than coming into the space for quiet activity and reflection.

We have a quote from the Environmental Trust, an organisation that specialises in working with schools to develop their green spaces. They have visited our school on two occasions and have prepared a plan for how we could develop this space.

The total amount of money we are applying for is £2400. We have received an award of £400 from Learning Through Landscapes that will contribute to this total.

A further grant would enable us to carry out the following work:
- Erect a wooden pergola with trellis, which would be attached to existing walls.
- Clad the central flowerbeds with lattice trellis to create visual interest and to allow trailing plants to grow up their sides.
- Create additional seating.
- Close off one entrance to the area and plant an interesting and decorative small tree at that point.
- Possibly put a curved seat around the tree.
- Establish more colourful and abundant planting with seasonal variations.
- Paint parts of the brickwork.

Pupils will take an active part in the project, working with the gardener to select a variety of plants and shrubs suitable for our flowerbeds. They will help to prepare for and plant these. Small groups of pupils with a lunchtime supervisor will be organised to water and care for the plants on a weekly basis. Members of the Playground Friends will use the area to sit with small groups of pupils, read them stories and play quiet games.

We believe the impact of a quiet zone will enable pupils to:
- develop their senses and stimulate their imagination and creativity in a pleasant, flourishing environment
- begin to recognise and respect the importance of the environment by caring for the plants and shrubs and by observing the wildlife (butterflies, ladybirds, ants, bees) that will be attracted to their garden

- develop a caring and nurturing attitude, which will enable them to respond appropriately to their surrounding space
- identify and recognise the importance of quiet reflection on their own or with others
- enhance their own feelings of wellbeing and self-worth by spending time in pleasant surroundings.

Although we have made many improvements to our playground, there is very little green space and no suitable seating area. When children sit in this area at the moment they are disturbed because other children tend to use it as a thoroughfare. The redevelopment planned will make the area more inviting to the children. They will then have a pleasing, colourful environment to spend time in. It will also be more welcoming to parents and visitors to the school, who will see how the school is improving the quality of the children's play space. Parents will be able to use the space as a meeting place at the beginning and end of the school day.

In the past year we have completed many of our key objectives for our Playground Action Plan.

We have:
- developed clear playground and game markings
- painted a mural, designed by the pupils with the help of a local artist, on the shed
- set up a Friendship Stop, a seating area where lonely or unhappy children can go and sit to be helped by the Playground Friends
- developed the Playground Friends, a group of pupils with special responsibilities who befriend lonely pupils, teach games and help to put the playground equipment away
- raised the status of the lunchtime supervisors by developing a playground reward and sanction system in line with our whole-school behaviour policy
- instituted regular meetings with supervisors to discuss issues and concerns.

We hope you will consider us favourably for this grant and we look forward to hearing from you.

Yours sincerely

Mandy Wilson
Head teacher

Enc.:   *Playground Action Plan*

St John's Primary School

Carling Road Cambridge CB6 7PQ

Mrs P. Jones
82 Barclay Close
Cambridge
CB5 8TV

20 April 2001

Dear Mrs Jones

I enclose our application form for funding for our lunchtime clubs.

These lunchtime clubs are a key element of the Quality Circle Time model, which is a whole-school approach to self-esteem building and positive behaviour management that is being implemented in our school. The funding we are applying for will be used to develop a lunchtime drama club within this framework. I enclose a copy of the overall Playground Action Plan of which the lunchtime groups are an integral part.

The drama club will consist of two mixed-ability groups with up to 12 children in each, and will include pupils with emotional and behavioural difficulties, alongside other pupils who will act as positive role models (within the school roll of 280, 70% of pupils are entitled to free school meals and 50% have been identified as having Special Educational Needs). The club would be run twice a week with the support of a project coordinator and assistant. It would be delivered within a clear framework encouraging cooperation and promoting a set of values that will help to build a safe, friendly and non-judgemental environment.

We recognise that having put in place clear strategies and resources to encourage good behaviour and a caring playtime ethos, there are some pupils who will not manage this without becoming involved in fights and other conflict situations. The drama club will be a proactive way to address these issues by helping pupils learn strategies to enable them to become more confident and valued members of our school community. If these issues are not addressed we believe that behaviour during playtime and class time will continue to deteriorate and that pupils could be at risk of lunchtime exclusion.

In our first year this project would benefit between 40 and 70 pupils. The programme for individuals would range from a six-week to a whole-year programme, depending on the individual pupil's needs and interests.

In summary, our outcomes at the end of the first year would be for pupils to:
- feel good about themselves
- develop conflict resolution strategies
- use drama strategies to 'put yourself in someone else's shoes'
- compliment each other and learn to give constructive criticism
- develop social skills to form and maintain positive relationships
- work cooperatively with others
- be able to express feelings within a safe, supportive and creative environment
- work towards projects which reflect personal experiences such as bullying, unhappiness, violence, friendship, dreams and aspirations
- have opportunities to show work in assemblies
- learn to cooperate with each other by preparing and performing their work
- learn to use improvisation techniques
- celebrate their own and other people's successes
- have fun.

We see the drama club as a very important part of our Playground Action Plan. We are working within a clear framework to establish a system which will empower our pupils and offer them opportunities to achieve, not only in academic terms but also by developing strong foundations for the continuing development of their life skills.

We hope you will consider supporting us in this project and we look forward to hearing from you.

Yours sincerely

Mandy Wilson
Head teacher

Enc.: Playground Action Plan

PLAYGROUND ACTION PLAN: ST JOHN'S PRIMARY SCHOOL

Key issue: Improve the playground environment   **Objective:** Improve the status of the supervisors

Action	Resources	Person responsible	Monitored by	Cost	Review date
• Develop a system to enable supervisors to have access to similar rewards and sanctions to those of the class teachers	• mini-certificates or notelets • monitoring forms • stickers • playground behaviour books	Mandy Wilson	Georgia Thorp Greg Brown	£50	Autumn term 2000
• Produce a booklet for parents on the school's playtime and lunchtime policy	• budget for production, including paper and photocopying	Mandy Wilson	Georgia Thorp Greg Brown	£50	Autumn term 2000
• Have regular team meetings with the supervisors and the coordinator to address key issues	• budgets to pay supervisor and coordinator for half-termly or monthly Circle Time meeting	Mandy Wilson	Georgia Thorp Greg Brown	£500	Autumn term 2000
• Provide appropriate training for the lunchtime supervisors to develop behaviour-management strategies in line with the school policy	• behaviour management training sessions	Mandy Wilson	Georgia Thorp Greg Brown	£300	Autumn term 2000

→

PLAYGROUND ACTION PLAN: ST JOHN'S PRIMARY SCHOOL

Key issue: Improve the playground environment   **Objective:** Develop clear markings for the zoned activity areas and display the Golden Playground Rules

Action	Resources	Person responsible	Monitored by	Cost	Review date
• Mark out the zoned areas	• budget for an artist to work with the children to design and paint the markings • paint	Mandy Wilson	Georgia Thorp Greg Brown	(see zone 3 below)	Autumn term 2000
• Display the Golden Playground Rules in all the zoned areas	• laminated copies of the playground rules	Mandy Wilson	Georgia Thorp Greg Brown	£20	Spring term 2001

Key issue: Improve the playground environment   **Objective:** Identify an area for planting trees

Action	Resources	Person responsible	Monitored by	Cost	Review date
• Continue to work with a local charity, who will provide funding for trees and shrubs in the grounds	• trees and shrubs			Nil	Spring term 2001

Key issue: Improve the playground environment   **Objective:** Improve the nursery play area

Action	Resources	Person responsible	Monitored by	Cost	Review date
• Develop the nursery play area with interactive wooden furniture/sculptures	• wooden furniture and sculptures			£500	Spring term 2001

→

Key issue: Improve the playground environment   **Objective:** Divide the playground into zoned activity areas

Action	Resources	Person responsible	Monitored by	Cost	Review date
Zone 1 ● Develop a quiet area using the garden at the front of the school ● Establish a no-through route in the area to minimise the 'traffic' of children ● Have a selection of books, magazines and puzzles for quiet activities ● Develop a rota system in which the Playground Friends sign up to read stories to some of the children in this area	● books ● puzzles ● magazines ● store cupboard ● large plant to create a no-through route	Mandy Wilson	Georgia Thorp Greg Brown	£100	Summer term 2001
Zone 2 ● Develop a stage area for putting on plays and having a dressing-up area	● dressing-up clothes ● storage box ● large wooden box painted in bright colours for stage	Mandy Wilson	Georgia Thorp Greg Brown	£200	Summer term 2001

→

PLAYGROUND ACTION PLAN: ST JOHN'S PRIMARY SCHOOL

Key issue: Improve the playground environment   **Objective:** Divide the playground into zoned activity areas

Action	Resources	Person responsible	Monitored by	Cost	Review date
Zone 3 • One shed will be part of the craze of the week area, where different games will be played – this will include the area with game markings	• an artist to paint and design the game markings, and work with children on a theme to paint the shed • french skipping elastics • skipping ropes • instructions for games printed on laminated cards • 'the craze of the week is …' board	Mandy Wilson	Georgia Thorp Greg Brown	Estimate £3000 (for all the artist's work) £150 (for playground equipment)	Spring term 2001
Zone 4 • Develop a football area • Develop a football parliament to make decisions on how to develop the use of the football space effectively and fairly	• helper/teacher to spend time developing work with the parliament • pitch markings	Mandy Wilson	Georgia Thorp Greg Brown	£100	Summer term 2001
Zone 5 • Develop a ball-skills area using cones for practising and learning ball skills	• cones • balls	Mandy Wilson	Georgia Thorp Greg Brown	£50	Summer term 2001

Key issue: Improve the playground environment   **Objective:** Divide the playground into zoned activity areas

Action	Resources	Person responsible	Monitored by	Cost	Review date
Zone 6 ● The existing shed in this area is being used for painting, playing with a dolls' house and construction kits. The area will have benches and tables and will also include game markings. This space will also be suitable for parents to sit and wait for their children after school.	● an artist to paint and design the game markings and work with some children on a theme to paint the shed ● 4 to 5 benches ● 4 to 5 tables ● easels ● paints and brushes ● dolls' house ● chalk ● construction kits	Mandy Wilson	Georgia Thorp Greg Brown	(see zone 3 above) £1000	Summer term 2001
Friendship Stop ● Buy a bench where lonely or unhappy children can sit and be befriended by the Playground Friends.	● bench ● Friendship Stop	Mandy Wilson	Georgia Thorp Greg Brown	£150	Summer term 2001

→

PLAYGROUND ACTION PLAN: ST JOHN'S PRIMARY SCHOOL

Key issue: Improve the playground environment   **Objective:** Develop a Community Taskforce

Action	Resources	Person responsible	Monitored by	Cost	Review date
Community Taskforce • Employ someone at lunchtimes to work with a small group of children on a variety of projects. The group would include children who are positive role models and children who find it difficult to manage playtimes without becoming involved in fights and other conflict situations. The projects that they work on might include: ▲ sanding down and varnishing old furniture ▲ making items such as pencil holders ▲ decorating boxes to be sold to raise money for the playground.	• budget for an additional member of staff and coordinator to manage the project • old furniture to restore • sandpaper • glue • suitable varnish • cardboard boxes to decorate • paper/pens/paints	Mandy Wilson	Georgia Thorp Greg Brown	£5000	Summer term 2001

12 | *A last word*

Be realistic, you can't change everything overnight. Make your action plan achievable for your school.

Take people on board with you. This is a journey for which you need many companions.

Be prepared to monitor and review constantly what you have done and to be open to reflect and change where necessary.

Be patient, this is not a quick fix. Small changes that become embedded in your school culture will gradually make a significant improvement.

Photocopiable materials

I am pleased with you because you chose to:

- ☐ 1. show good manners
- ☐ 2. be helpful
- ☐ 3. refuse to be drawn into a fight
- ☐ 4. play well with other children
- ☐ 5. queue patiently
- ☐ 6. ask someone to join in a game.

Name ……….......…………………..

Class ……………… Date …..………

Supervisor ……………………..

I am pleased with you because you chose to:

- ☐ 1. show good manners
- ☐ 2. be helpful
- ☐ 3. refuse to be drawn into a fight
- ☐ 4. play well with other children
- ☐ 5. queue patiently
- ☐ 6. ask someone to join in a game.

Name ……….......…………………..

Class ……………… Date …..………

Supervisor ……………………..

I am pleased with you because you chose to:

- ☐ 1. show good manners
- ☐ 2. be helpful
- ☐ 3. refuse to be drawn into a fight
- ☐ 4. play well with other children
- ☐ 5. queue patiently
- ☐ 6. ask someone to join in a game.

Name ……….......…………………..

Class ……………… Date …..………

Supervisor ……………………..

I am pleased with you because you chose to:

- ☐ 1. show good manners
- ☐ 2. be helpful
- ☐ 3. refuse to be drawn into a fight
- ☐ 4. play well with other children
- ☐ 5. queue patiently
- ☐ 6. ask someone to join in a game.

Name ……….......…………………..

Class ……………… Date …..………

Supervisor ……………………..

PLAYGROUND MONITORING FORM

I am pleased with you

Date	Name/Class	Rule kept	Reported by

1. have shown good manners
2. have been helpful
3. refused to be drawn into a fight
4. played well with other children
5. queued patiently
6. asked someone to join in a game.

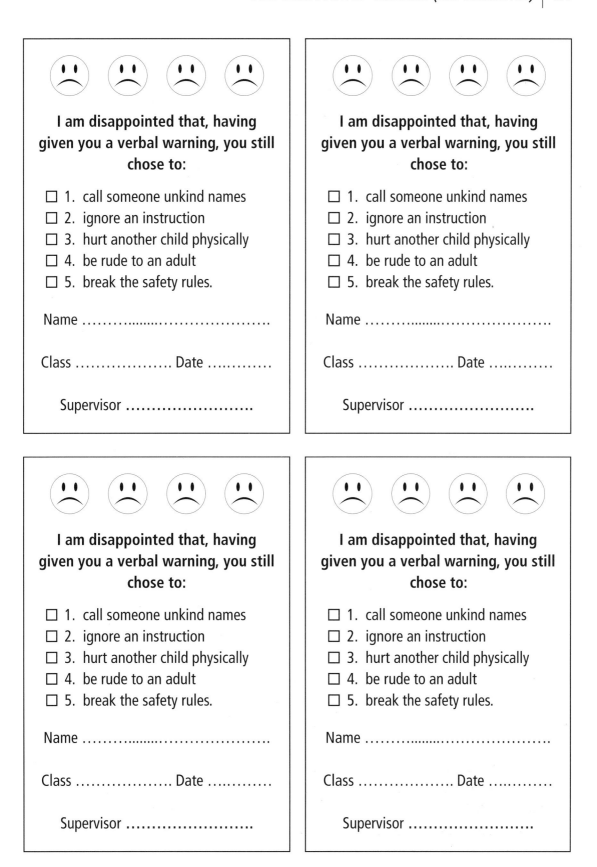

I am disappointed that, having given you a verbal warning, you still chose to:

☐ 1. call someone unkind names
☐ 2. ignore an instruction
☐ 3. hurt another child physically
☐ 4. be rude to an adult
☐ 5. break the safety rules.

Name ……….......…..................

Class ……………… Date ….………

Supervisor ……………………..

I am disappointed that, having given you a verbal warning, you still chose to:

☐ 1. call someone unkind names
☐ 2. ignore an instruction
☐ 3. hurt another child physically
☐ 4. be rude to an adult
☐ 5. break the safety rules.

Name ……….......…..................

Class ……………… Date ….………

Supervisor ……………………..

I am disappointed that, having given you a verbal warning, you still chose to:

☐ 1. call someone unkind names
☐ 2. ignore an instruction
☐ 3. hurt another child physically
☐ 4. be rude to an adult
☐ 5. break the safety rules.

Name ……….......…..................

Class ……………… Date ….………

Supervisor ……………………..

I am disappointed that, having given you a verbal warning, you still chose to:

☐ 1. call someone unkind names
☐ 2. ignore an instruction
☐ 3. hurt another child physically
☐ 4. be rude to an adult
☐ 5. break the safety rules.

Name ……….......…..................

Class ……………… Date ….………

Supervisor ……………………..

PLAYGROUND MONITORING FORM
I am disappointed with your behaviour

Date	Name/Class	Rule kept	Reported by

1. called someone unkind names
2. ignored an instruction
3. hurt another child physically

4. were rude to an adult
5. broke the safety rules.

Playground targets

This must be signed by a supervisor after each playtime.

A smiley face means I have kept my targets.

A sad face means I have not kept my targets.

When I get .... smiley faces, I will go and see .... and a 'Well done' certificate will be sent home.

If I get .... sad faces, I will go and see .... and a letter will be sent home.

Name ....

Date ....

My playground targets are:

1 _____
_____
_____

2 _____
_____
_____

3 _____
_____
_____

Playground targets

This must be signed by a supervisor after each playtime.

A smiley face means I have kept my targets.

A sad face means I have not kept my targets.

When I get .... smiley faces, I will go and see .... and a 'Well done' certificate will be sent home.

If I get .... sad faces, I will go and see .... and a letter will be sent home.

Name ....

Date ....

My playground targets are:

1 _____
_____
_____

2 _____
_____
_____

3 _____
_____
_____

To be used for the back of the playground target sheet (see page 175)

Dear ....

I am really pleased with

....

    for:

    🙂 keeping their playground targets

From .... Date ....

WELL DONE

Dear ....

I am really pleased with

....

    for:

    🙂 keeping their playground targets

From .... Date ....

WELL DONE

YOUR SCHOOL

NEEDS

YOU!

Are you a good friend?

Do you keep your cool under pressure?

Do you like to help others in need?

Would you like to make a difference to your school?

APPLY TO BE A PLAYGROUND FRIEND NOW.

Ask for a form at the school office.

Application form for

....

Name .... Date .... Class ....

Why would you like to do this job?

....

....

PLEASE TICK ALL THE JOBS YOU ARE INTERESTED IN DOING

- [ ] help teach playground games
- [ ] help lonely children make friends
- [ ] help put out and collect playtime equipment
- [ ] help in the dining hall.

You will need to
★ be kind and not bossy
★ wear a special uniform
★ have meetings with ....

At the end of half-term you will get
★ a special certificate in assembly
★ a special surprise reward.

Thank you for filling this in.

Please return it to ....

by ....

The .... Team ....

Put your name down for the different jobs this week

Monday	Name	Name	Name	Name	Name
craze of the week					
traditional games					
collecting the equipment					
dining hall duty					
Friendship Stop duty					
Tuesday					
craze of the week					
traditional games					
collecting the equipment					
dining hall duty					
Friendship Stop duty					
Wednesday					
craze of the week					
traditional games					
collecting the equipment					
dining hall duty					
Friendship Stop duty					
Thursday					
craze of the week					
traditional games					
collecting the equipment					
dining hall duty					
Friendship Stop duty					
Friday					
craze of the week					
traditional games					
collecting the equipment					
dining hall duty					
Friendship Stop duty					

Team ...
Supervisor ...

1 ....

2 ....

3 ....

4 ....

5 ....

6 ....

7 ....

8 ....

9 ....

10 ....

11 ....

12 ....

To ....

'Well done' for:

- ☆ Walking away from trouble
- ☆ Letting someone play a game with you
- ☆ Putting the games away
- ☆ Being kind to someone

From ....

Date ....

To ....

'Well done' for:

- ☆ Walking away from trouble
- ☆ Letting someone play a game with you
- ☆ Putting the games away
- ☆ Being kind to someone

From ....

Date ....

To ....

'Well done' for:

- ☆ Walking away from trouble
- ☆ Letting someone play a game with you
- ☆ Putting the games away
- ☆ Being kind to someone

From ....

Date ....

To ....

'Well done' for:

- ☆ Walking away from trouble
- ☆ Letting someone play a game with you
- ☆ Putting the games away
- ☆ Being kind to someone

From ....

Date ....

Name .... Class ....

What do you like about being a Playground Friend?

_____

_____

What jobs do you do as a Playground Friend?

_____

_____

How does being a Playground Friend make you feel?

_____

_____

What ideas do you have to help make you a better Playground Friend?

_____

_____

What don't you like about being a Playground Friend?

_____

_____

Is there any training you would like to help you improve how you do your job?

_____

_____

Name

....

I am a

....

Date started

....

I am on duty on

....

1

Understanding and managing our angry feelings

Here are some safe ways of managing your angry feelings without hurting yourself, others or property. Add any more you can think of to the list.

- run around the playground
- count to 10 slowly
- have time out
- find someone to talk to
- read a book
- write down your feelings
- calm down before you talk about it
- use 'I' statements to say how you feel

....

....

....

....

8

Understanding and managing our angry feelings

Anger is a strong emotion, and it's OK to feel angry.

Write down some things that make you angry.

....

....

....

What happens to your body when you are angry?

....

....

....

What do you do when you are angry?

....

....

7

Rules, responsibilities and routines

I wanted to join because:

....

....

The rules for our group are:

....

....

....

These are our playground rules and safety routines:

....

....

....

2

Rules, responsibilities and routines

I am responsible for:

....

....

....

My responsibilities to do with my uniform are:

....

....

My responsibilities to do with the playground equipment are:

....

....

My responsibilities at our meetings are:

....

....

3

'I' statements

We can practise saying how we feel and what we want without blaming anyone by using 'I' statements.

Practise finishing off these sentences.

I feel .... (sad, annoyed, angry, disappointed)

When ....

....
(say what happened)

Because ....
(say why)

I would like to/I want to ....

....
(what you want to happen or to change)

Remember you won't always get what you want, but you have spoken to the other person with respect and said how you feel and what you want. It helps if you can work with the other person to try to find something you can both agree on.

6

Good communication and cooperation

To communicate and cooperate with others we need to have certain qualities and learn some skills.

We need to:
- be friendly
- be kind
- speak gently
- listen to the other person
- ask them how they feel.

We also need to:

....

....

....

The skills and qualities I have are:

....

....

....

....

4

Good communication and cooperation

What do you need to practise?

I need to practise:

....

....

....

....

What sort of questions could you ask a child who may be lonely?

....

....

....

....

....

5

Lunchtime audit

The aim of this questionnaire is to identify and focus on particular areas we need to work on to improve our lunchtime system.

1. How long does it take the children from lining up to sitting down and eating their lunch?

2. How long does it take from the children arriving into the dining hall to leaving?

3. Are there any bottlenecks in lines during this time?
   If yes, where are they?

4. What conflict situations occur in the queues?

5. What conflict situations occur at the tables?

6. Do we have a distinct set of dining rules that is displayed clearly in the dining hall?

7. How are children encouraged to keep the lunchtime rules?

8. Do we have appropriate rewards and sanctions for the dining hall that comply with our behaviour policy?

9. How are children treated in the dining hall by members of staff?

10. How do the children treat staff?

11. How do the children treat each other?

12. How are good manners encouraged?

Football Rules Contract

If you would like to play football and agree with the football rules that we have written together, sign your name below.

(If you do not sign you will not be allowed to play!)

Class ....

● ●

Names

....

....

....

....

....

....

....

....

....

....

To ....

For ....

....

Date ....

To ....

For ....

....

Date ....

To ....

For ....

....

Date ....

To ....

For ....

....

Date ....

To ....

For ....

....

Date ....

To ....

For ....

....

Date ....

To ....

For ....

....

Date ....

To ....

For ....

....

Date ....

To ....

For ....

....

Date ....

To ....

For ....

....

Date ....

To ....

For ....

....

Date ....

To ....

For ....

....

Date ....

To ....

For ....

....

Date ....

To ....

For ....

....

Date ....

To ....

For ....

....

Date ....

To ....

For ....

....

Date ....

To ....

For ....

....

Date ....

To ....

For ....

....

Date ....

Playtime Policy

Staff, parents, pupils, governors and parents working together to make our playground and playtimes caring, creative and stimulating for everyone.

December 2001

Celebrating the Friendship Squad

- Every half-term we have a special assembly to discuss playtime rules and routines at which we publicly thank the Friendship Squad and award them a special certificate.
- At the end of the year we have a party or other celebration for the Friendship Squad.

Rules, rewards and sanctions

To encourage pupils to keep the rules we have developed a clear rewards and sanctions system that is used by all playground staff.

Our playground rules are:

- We listen to the adults in the playground.
- We stand still when the bell rings.
- We play together and look after each other.
- We let other children get on with their own games.
- We sort out our problems in a fair way.
- We give the equipment back to the Friendship Squad at the end of play.

Rewards

All supervisors have yellow 'I am pleased with you' mini-certificates that pupils may receive for a variety of reasons including:

- being kind to other children
- refusing to be drawn into a fight
- asking someone to join in a game.

Supervisors can give these directly to the class teacher or to individual children. Some classes link these directly with their class reward system.

Problem-solving

Staff try to help pupils sort out any problems in a fair way, encouraging pupils to take responsibility for their behaviour. They will listen to all parties involved and encourage pupils to find a fair solution that both parties can agree to.

Sanctions

If pupils are not able to sort out their problems in a fair way, continue to break the school rules, use aggressive or bullying behaviour, the following sanctions are used:

- The pupil's name is written on a red 'I am disappointed' notelet, outlining the rule they have broken.
- The notelet is put in a box in the head teacher's office.
- The head teacher speaks to the pupil.
- If the pupil's name appears in the box more than twice in a week playtime targets are set.
- If the problem continues a letter is sent home and help is sought from parents/carers.

Our playground policy has been developed by staff, governors, parents and pupils to help create a caring ethos in the playground, which is in line with our behaviour and anti-bullying policies.

Our aims are to:
• ensure that pupils are safe
• give pupils opportunities to develop their social skills through play and interaction in a stimulating and caring environment
• have a consistent and effective rewards and sanctions system
• encourage and support the pupils in the Friendship Squad
• employ a direct approach which focuses on the active role pupils take in problem-solving.

Daily activities in the playground

We have a selection of daily activities and resources to help pupils develop skills of cooperation and turn-taking.

The list of resources used each day is displayed in the playground, outside the office, in the dining hall and in each class. We have:
• skipping ropes
• stilts
• dressing-up clothes
• bats and balls
• hoops
• hoop-la.

• tape/CD player
• copies of traditional playground games printed on card (these are kept in the Friendship Squad's tray outside the office).

We have the following zoned activity areas:
Quiet zone: the garden area is used for quiet talking and reading
Football zone
Cricket zone: in the summer
Friendship Stop: this is a place where lonely pupils can sit and wait for someone in the Friendship Squad to come and talk to them.

We also have indoor lunchtime clubs.
At present we have:
• drama club
• music club.

The Friendship Squad

The Friendship Squad consists of pupils who apply to do jobs during playtimes in the playground and inside during wet playtimes, and in the dining hall. They wear tabards so they can be easily identified.

What do the Friendship Squad do?

Their jobs include:
• teaching children games
• befriending lonely children and helping them to make friends

• telling the supervisors if they have any concerns regarding playtimes, such as bullying and fighting
• helping to take out and put away playground equipment
• helping in the dining hall
• participating in training sessions to help them develop the skills they need to do their jobs well
• having their own mini-certificates that they can give out when they see acts of kindness, politeness and other good behaviour

Why do we need the Friendship Squad?

• The members are positive role models who teach the qualities of caring and friendship.
• They raise their own and other pupils' self-esteem.
• They help to create a positive ethos in our school.

Who supports the Friendship Squad?

All lunchtime supervisors support and encourage the members of the Friendship Squad during playtimes. Two supervisors have regular meetings to discuss routines and playtime issues with them.

Dear ....

Please come and visit us at playtime on:

Day ....

Time ....

Please let us know if you can come by ....
If you prefer to come on another day, please let us know.

From ....

Dear ....

Please come and visit us at playtime on:

Day ....

Time ....

Please let us know if you can come by ....
If you prefer to come on another day, please let us know.

From ....

PARENTS AS PARTNERS CERTIFICATE

We are proud to award

....

a Parents as Partners certificate for

....

....

Date ....

Signed ....

MASTER ACTION PLAN

Task	Have you:	Resources you may need	Person responsible/ monitored by	Estimated cost	Review date

Training and resources

Jenny Mosley INSET courses

The following courses and workshops are available from a team of highly qualified and experienced consultants, who can be contacted through:

Jenny Mosley Consultancies
8 Westbourne Road
Trowbridge
Wiltshire
BA14 0AJ

Tel: 01225 767157
Fax: 01225 755631
Email: circletime@jennymosley.demon.co.uk
Web site: www.circle-time.co.uk

- ▶ **Promoting happier lunchtimes**
- ▶ **Turn your school round – an introduction**
- ▶ **A whole-school approach to building self-esteem through Circle Time**
- ▶ **Assessing the effectiveness of your self-esteem, anti-bullying and positive behaviour policies**
- ▶ **Raising staff morale through team-building**
- ▶ **Practical activities to maintain and develop the power of Circle Time**
- ▶ **A workshop of games to enrich class and lunchtimes.**

Training support for your workplace

The Jenny Mosley Consultancies' well-trained personnel, experienced in all aspects of the Quality Circle Time model, are available to visit your workplace to give courses and workshops to all your teaching and support staff.

We run both closure and in-school days. In the closure day, all staff, teachers, teaching assistants, lunchtime supervisors and administrative staff are invited to explore how to develop team-building and moral values through Golden Rules, incentives and sanctions, and ideas for happier lunchtimes.

During the in-school day the school does not close and the Quality Circle Time method is demonstrated with whole classes of children, observed by a range of staff. In addition to this, Circle Time meetings are held for lunchtime supervisors and an action plan for the school is considered with key members of staff.

Training the trainer courses

Key people may be trained either to go back to their school or their LEA as accredited trainers, responsible for supporting all adults and children in their community through the Jenny Mosley model. For details of ongoing courses contact Jenny Mosley Consultancies on 01225 767157.

Quality Circle Time training manuals and resources

Mosley, J. (1998) *More Quality Circle Time*, LDA

Mosley, J. (1997) *Quality Circle Time*, LDA

Mosley, J. (1993) *Turn Your School Round*, LDA

Mosley, J. and Sonnet, H. (2002) *101 Games for Self-Esteem*, LDA

Mosley, J. and Sonnet, H. (2002) *Making Waves – Parachute games*, LDA

Mosley, J. and Thorp, G. (2002) *Playground Games*, LDA

Mosley, J. and Thorp, G. (2002) *Playground Notelets*, LDA

Goldthorpe, M. (1998) *Effective IEPs through Circle Time*, LDA

Goldthorpe, M. (1998) *Poems for Circle Time and Literacy Hour*, LDA

Goldthorpe, M. and Nutt, L. (2000) *Assemblies to Teach Golden Rules*, LDA

Mosley, J. (2000) *Quality Circle Time in Action,* LDA

Mosley, J. (2000) *Quality Circle Time Kit*, LDA

Mosley, J. (1996) *Class Reward Sheets*, LDA

Mosley, J. (1996) *Golden Rules Posters*, LDA

Mosley, J. (1996) *Responsibility Badges*, LDA

Mosley, J. (1996) *Reward Certificates*, LDA

Mosley, J. (1996) *Stickers*, LDA

For information about the full range of Jenny Mosley's books and resources, please ring LDA Customer Services on 01945 463441.